Teach me to write ... Fiction

A GUIDE FOR TEACHERS

Alan Gibbons

Nash Pollock Publishing

Acknowledgements

Many thanks to Carol Canavan, Catherine Carson, Linda Richardson, Phil Newton, Anne Gray, Steve Jorgensen, Bryan Wynne, everyone at Flintshire and Denbighshire LEAs, Angela Bradshaw and the Surrey English team, Maureen Pavey, Knowsley LEA, and all the youngsters I have worked with.

© Alan Gibbons

First published 2005
Published by
Nash Pollock Publishing
32 Warwick Street
Oxford OX4 1SX

Reprinted 2010

Orders to:
Nash Pollock Publishing
PO Box 150
Winsford
Cheshire
CW7 3WA

TEL: 01606 836699   FAX: 01606 836655
email: sales@nashpollock.co.uk

ISBN 10: 1 898255 45 8

ISBN 13: 978 1 898255 45 1

Design and typesetting by Black Dog Design, Buckingham
Printed in Great Britain by Berforts Ltd, Stevenage

Contents

PART 1

Introduction
Sitting in a wardrobe

The wardrobe

It all started with a wardrobe, 'it' being my love of reading, and the wardrobe being the venerable lump of furniture into which I fled to read *The Lion, the Witch and the Wardrobe* by C S Lewis in the hope that I too might force open the rear panel and journey into the fabled land of Narnia. I really did feel that, with a little bit of effort, I would be welcomed by Mr Tumnus into that snowy realm. That story, which I read when I was eight, was one of the first to help me understand that books are so much more than cardboard, paper and print. They are portals to other worlds, alternative ways of being. They give us the opportunity to empathise, to view the world through another person's eyes, to walk in their shoes, feel the beat of their heart and sense the rhythms and cadences of their feelings.

If there is one thing that makes a writer, it is reading. If you read for pleasure, then that which seems hard to the non-reader comes so much more easily. You absorb, almost by osmosis, that odd web of talents what it takes to write:
- sentence structure
- pacing and plotting
- tension
- timing
- aphorisms
- dialogue
- description
- imagery, metaphor and simile
- character development

It is a happy by-product that reading also teaches us the principles of grammar, the rules of spelling and the opportunities offered by a rich vocabulary, not by instruction but by being absorbed in a good story. We learn *in context*. I have never read fiction with the sole purpose of learning. I read for a much greater purpose, to be absorbed in a good story and transported to another place. But in reading I have always learned. In fact, like many people, I tend to learn better by myself, curled up with a book, than with other people being instructed. So what was it that set me on the road to being a literate child, and later an adult who ended up earning his living as a writer? Well, it was enjoyment, basically.

I loved sitting with my mother, becoming immersed in a favourite story. I adored 'Listen with Mother' on BBC Radio, even if the presenters' cultured home counties voices were quite different from my own Cheshire accent, exotic even. Maybe it was part of the fascination that they spoke so differently from my own family. I have never been put off by diversity. In that otherness I found riches. There were many other examples of quality speaking and listening experiences in my childhood. My grandmother told me family legends. One that sticks in my mind is how, if there was a family quarrel, my great grandmother, a forbidding Irish matriarch, would march to the back door and hurl the poker down the yard.

'Now, if you don't stop,' she would say, 'I'll go and get that poker and there will be hell to pay.' She never needed to get the poker.

Gran also wove tales about her favourite movie stars and I lapped up *Oliver Twist*, *The Great Escape*, *South Pacific*, *Great Expectations*, *Kind Hearts and Coronets*, *Dracula*, *Wuthering Heights* and *Spartacus* on film. Sad as it may seem, once when I had suffered a particularly unpleasant and persistent bout of bullying I dreamed of thousands of the other boys rising one after the other to announce in defiance of my tormentors: 'I am Alan Gibbons!' It didn't happen, of course. I had to learn to fight my own battles. When I was ten I heard Martin Luther King's 'I have a dream' speech. The hairs on the back of my neck still rise at the memory of such sublime oratory. About the same time I heard John Lennon's acerbic wit. His rebellious persona in the movie *A Hard Day's Night* had me and my mates running round Crewe town centre like lunatics. The spoken word, I realised, was rich and engaging beyond belief.

In school I was further entranced by the best of my teachers who, during story-time, introduced me to, among others, *Emil and the Detectives*, *Treasure Island*, *Lorna Doone*, *She*, *Bows Against the Barons*, *Animal Farm*, *Uncle Tom's Cabin*, *1984* and *My Family and Other Animals*.

In other words a chain of events was set in motion which went something like this:
• Good quality speaking and listening experiences led to good quality reading experiences
• Good quality reading experiences led to good quality writing experiences.

Of course, not everything that happened to me during my education was positive. This was the unforgiving fifties and sixties when some teachers ruled with a rod of iron and a tongue dripping with sarcasm. Several of my teachers fit the description Nike Man. Their guidance to their class: 'Just do it.' They gave a short stimulus and left you to it, administering the lesson from their desk at the front of the classroom. If you were a reader you could cope. You had, after all, internalised models of writing which acted as a template for your own work. If you weren't a reader, you didn't. There were many times I felt pretty disenchanted with school life but a reservoir of affection for speaking and listening, reading and writing was created from which I continue to draw today.

The challenge

That brings me to the purpose of this book. I am now a full-time writer and independent literacy consultant. I spent nearly twenty years as a junior and infant teacher in Merseyside. Later I worked as author in residence at Prescot and Simonswood primary schools and for Knowsley LEA, working in some fifty primary and secondary schools on the eastern rim of Merseyside, an area of very substantial social deprivation. Most of the children's writing featured in this book comes from workshops I have led. I now visit over 150 schools and libraries a year. I also provide in-service training for teachers in the UK and abroad. On my travels I soon started to realise that teachers are continually told *what* to teach, but rarely *how* to. All too often teachers are expected to transform the requirements set out in an abstract, sometimes very nearly unreadable, document into quality teaching. What they really need to see is the process and the product.

Here are some questions which crop up in discussion after discussion:
• How do I structure my teaching of writing?
• What do I tell the children to do? How much guidance do they need?
• What is the balance between prescription and creativity?
• What does a good piece of work look like?
• How can I ensure progression?

This is my attempt to offer one educator's perspective on writing. I don't pretend to have come up with the last word in good practice. That is the whole point: in literature there is no last word. Landmark books such as Robert Swindells' *Stone Cold*, Robert Cormier's *The Chocolate War*, Mark Haddon's *The Curious Incident of the Dog in the Night Time*, Philip Pullman's 'His Dark Materials' trilogy, Kevin Crossley-Holland's 'Arthur' trilogy, Malorie Blackman's *Noughts and Crosses* or David Almond's *Skellig* are original. They re-write the script, reconfigure the imaginative landscape.

That doesn't mean teachers should just throw up their hands in abject surrender and wait for the more able of their charges to be inspired by such models and *just create*. That is abdication. If there is one group of children which is often ignored in our education system it is the children of average ability. But they are the majority of children. As adults they will form the backbone of our society. If you set aside the gifted minority, let's face it, most children can't *just create*. They need a measure of help and guidance to learn how to express themselves successfully in writing. Absolute prescription doesn't work either. Teaching by numbers, often attempted in recent years, confines creativity and dulls imagination. It stops children wanting to write. What good teachers can do is demonstrate structures, frameworks, templates and pathways to the young writer, while leaving space for choices.

There has never been a more pressing need for good English teaching. There are all sorts of pressures on young people's lives. Social dislocation, family breakdown and child poverty can have a devastating impact on young people, making them miserable and depressed or dulling their appetite for learning. The pressure of too many examinations can squeeze all enjoyment out of school life, and never have children had to undergo so many tests and examinations. Then there are those other demands on their leisure time, so often derided by teachers and the press – TV and computer games. I would argue that watching TV or playing computer games are not that harmful in themselves. Bright, literate children tend to do both. It is uncritical viewing and playing, pursuing these activities to the exclusion of everything else, which is dangerous. Add to all these factors the power of peer pressure – the view that it's not cool to be 'a boffin' – and the journey to educational success can seem arduous, if not epic.

For the reasons detailed above and others, the habit of reading for pleasure has been squeezed in young people's lives. When it comes to cutbacks in public expenditure, libraries and book provision are often the first things for the chop. I referred to a chain earlier: good quality speaking and listening leads to good quality reading; good quality reading leads to good quality writing. When the links in the chain are cut for any reason it becomes extremely difficult to develop good writing. I will never forget the young boy who began his show-and-tell with the immortal words: 'Yer know worra mean like.' I had to explain patiently that I didn't because he hadn't told me yet!

The question here is blindingly obvious. How do you write a readable sentence when much of the communication around you falls short of forming coherent units of meaning?

That brings me to the scale of the problem. Ofsted reports have indicated that about half of all boys, for example, start secondary school without having achieved the average Level 4 in writing. A large, and little discussed, minority of girls have similar problems. Nobody can be complacent about standards of literacy.

The literate classroom

So what can be done? To start with, we can create a literate environment for the learner. Do you, the teacher, read for pleasure? If the answer is yes, then you shouldn't hide the fact. In fact, you should broadcast it from the rooftops. Have covers of some of your favourite books on display. Be seen reading. In the early years, tell stories and not just from a book. Have the confidence to memorise and perform stories with a recognisable pattern and structure. Watch good comedians and learn how to 'work an audience'. The teacher who enthrals their pupils with oral tales and anecdotes from their own lives is demonstrating how to narrate, to weave patterns of language which thrill, engage and entertain. A teacher shouldn't be an impersonal educating machine constantly plugged into her laptop, but a charismatic good example of how to be human. Anything less lets our children down.

Further up the school, have a sustained, silent reading time when they see you do it and do it themselves. Everyone, from the head teacher (yes, you lead the school so switch off that PC for fifteen minutes and set an example!) to the cook, the caretaker and the parent helpers should take part. Tell the pupils about your own reading. Finally, look for opportunities for reading and writing across the curriculum, in history, geography, PSHE and RE. There is more than one way to skin the literacy cat. Mind you, when it comes right down to it, if the answer to the question posed earlier is no, you don't read for pleasure, are you quite sure you're in the right job?

Now let's look at the children themselves. Do we expect the pupils to be readers? Is the school library attractive and inviting? Is there a school librarian tailoring the children's reading to their interests? Just imagine the effect of a well-informed adult taking small groups of children into the library to inspect and choose from a selection of attractive fiction. This is the direction the library service should surely take, intensive, interventionist Reader Development. The numbers reading for pleasure could be expanded substantially. In my opinion a professional librarian is essential to the development of literacy in a school. One great educational reform would be to provide a librarian for every high school and one for every cluster of four or five primary schools. Otherwise, where is the expertise to come from? Who will read *Books for Keeps* and *Carousel*, the book magazines, and make informed book purchases? Who will log onto Achuka, the internet site specialising in books for young people, and engage in the current debates about children's literature? Who will direct the child who wants to be a writer to the invaluable *Young Writer* magazine?

Is the best in recent children's fiction prominently displayed? Are there posters of writers on the walls? Finally, is there a 'Book of the Week' slot introduced by an enthusiastic young reader?

As any teacher knows, the child who reads for pleasure is a successful child. So let's produce more of them. A little investment in books and expertise goes a very long way. Double the number of children who read for pleasure in a school, and you will transform the whole attitude to learning. Plus you can be sure standards – and test results – will rise.

So how can you do it? First, book purchasing by the school is vital. Children will not be encouraged to read if the school library is an afterthought, if the shelves are stocked with ageing, tired-looking volumes. Somebody has to take responsibility for making the school a book-centred environment. That means investment, both in fixed resources and people. Priorities have to be set, and there is no greater priority than book provision. Initiatives such as reading volunteer schemes are invaluable. Parents and that great untapped resource, grandparents, coming in to read to, and with, children can have a tremendous impact.

Book ownership too is crucial. Every school should have regular book fairs. There should be a school bookshop from which children can order and buy the latest 'happening' books as well as the much-loved classics, or simply the unknown gems which take their fancy. Every school should have at least one visit a year from a poet, novelist or non-fiction writer to raise the profile of reading. Meeting a writer can have a huge impact. Previous non-readers' pleasure in reading can be massively enhanced by meeting a writer. Finally, the school should make a real effort to persuade those parents who are not convinced, that their child should have their own small library at home.

Now let's consider the links in the chain: good quality speaking and listening leading to good quality reading; good quality reading leading to good quality writing. All the foundations for good quality literacy experiences are laid in the early years. Here is one recent example from St Joseph's Primary, Huyton, Merseyside. I started by telling the children in Year 1 an oral story, 'Down at Zombie Joe's'. They chanted the chorus with appropriate hand gestures. Yes, whisper it, but we started with *fun*. Choral story-telling is always popular. The story goes like this:

Down at Zombie Joe's

There are rusty gates and creaking hinges.
Down at Zombie Joe's.
You walk through an overgrown garden where strange creatures lurk.
Down at Zombie Joe's.

There are big, black bats and slimy rats.
Down at Zombie Joe's.
When you go indoors there are snarling beasts.
Down at Zombie Joe's.
Floorboards creak and beasties squeak.
Down at Zombie Joe's.
Back outside the gravestones sag in the cracking earth.
Down at Zombie Joe's.
What's that wriggling shape? Could it be a monstrous head?
Down at Zombie Joe's.
Eyes stare at you with a hungry look.
Down at Zombie Joe's.
Don't hang around. Run for your life.
Down at Zombie Joe's.
Get out fast or you'll never escape. You'll always be there.
Down at Zombie Joe's.

It is vital that story-time is established as an activity which is exciting and is, to some extent, an end in itself. Not every story or poem has to be pulled apart, analysed and examined. Develop story time as an oasis of pleasure and you will soon have the children asking for their favourites. In the case of 'Down at Zombie Joe's' an activity did follow. The children were given a sheet of A4 paper split into four. They went away and sequenced the story they had heard by drawing pictures (see Figure 1). Through discussion and demonstration the teacher helped them work out what went in each section so that the story progressed.

The next stage would be to discuss with the children in groups how they could tell their stories to the rest of the class using these story boards as a prompt. The teacher could photocopy a selection of stories onto overhead projection transparencies and have the children tell their stories while they are projected onto a screen behind them. In this way the children are valued as authors. They have an audience.

The teacher could then, in a future lesson, reproduce a sample story board, blowing it up to A3 size, and show the children how to write a sentence underneath, each picture matching the pictures. The class could then read the story together. Even if the children are not yet fluent readers, the cumulative nature of the experience and the shortness of the text mean that they will all be able to join in and make the vital links. The final stage would be to give the individual children a new sheet. This time they would draw their pictures and, with adult help, write a sentence to match each picture. The connection

Figure 1

8

between this sort of activity and an appreciation of good quality picture books is self-evident (see Figure 2).

In this way the link between listening to a story, re-telling it, reading it and writing it can be established. In this sequence of lessons, the teacher is demonstrating the sentence as the basic unit of narrative, showing concretely what coherent units of meaning are and helping young children to reproduce them. Each activity informs the next in a progressive sequence of lessons. In this way a pattern can be set for the future.

Speaking and listening, reading and writing are not seen as sealed, separate activities but as three elements in a consistent, cumulative, holistic approach to literacy.

The approach

I don't subscribe to any one particular method of teaching writing. At the grammar school I attended as a boy, as I reminisced earlier, the predominant method was Nike Man teaching: 'Just do it.' When I started teaching, creativity was the watchword. An enthusiastic teacher would urge her pupils to approach the Curver box she had brought in. 'Gather round, children,' she would say. 'There is something special in my box. Touch it, feel it, experience it. Yes, it's a conch shell. Now where would you go with your magic conch shell?' The only problem is that the lesson ended up following the same pattern as that of the grammar school teacher of the nineteen sixties. The children would be introduced to a stimulus, then be expected to create with little support or guidance.

Now I'm too long in the tooth to fall for zealotry or experts bearing gifts, but there are ways to stimulate young writers and sustain their interest in the writing process. Sure, there are no quick fixes. Take a look at the approach for which I have been arguing. Firstly, teachers act as exemplars, sharing their love of reading, involving the children in enjoyable activities based on story. This depends to a great extent on teachers having the time to accumulate thorough subject knowledge, to read, and to use that reading to inform their teaching of reading and writing. They will then establish a literate classroom in a literate school, encouraging larger numbers of pupils to read for pleasure and use their reading to model their writing. Finally they will encourage good quality writing developing out of a curriculum rich in speaking, listening and personalised reading.

Once all this is set in motion, it is possible to 'scaffold' the young people's writing, guiding them through the activity in bite-sized segments of teaching with clear short-term objectives.

0

I went in to the scirree house. It had a mowrh for a bore. and it had sum funder and litning withe All dots srownding It.

2

I tiptad up the stirrs and I saw a gost and I ran down agen. It was a tine gost and All guing on its fays ond in bad Red hare.

4

I saw somtey tons I Ran as fast as my legs cud tack my and finley I stapt to a stop and I got home

3

I creept in to the garden and I saw a gray ston. I crepd close and close and close as I saw a hand creep ot. ov the gadn and I crepd

Figure 2

All this takes time and you have to make priorities. You can't expect expertise in English if teachers are so overwhelmed with paperwork, target-setting and number-crunching that they can't read a range of literature. As I have travelled around the UK I have noticed a remarkable unevenness. I have sat in staff rooms and English departments where not one teacher seems to read for pleasure. In others almost everyone does. We have to raise the weakest to the level of the strongest. An integrated approach is an indispensable and sure foundation for the teaching of English. On this solid foundation we can suggest some elements which seem to work:

- Lessons led by relaxed, confident teachers who have enough leisure time to read. This is not a dream. I have been part of such an environment.
- Lessons with pace.
- Lessons with humour.
- Lessons that are scaffolded with short term objectives so that the child knows what they are doing next and feels secure in their learning.
- Lessons with purpose. By purpose I mean this: does the child feel her writing is valued? Is there an audience out there to read it?

To ensure that a child's writing is read, we can:
- Display work throughout the school, not just in the classroom. There has been something of a trend in a number of schools to replace children's work with lists of connectives or adjectives. This is a backward step. Yes, have various aide-memoires for the pupils but on this condition: that there is plenty of children's work demonstrating how those connectives or adjectives are employed in context.
- Make attractive anthologies of work which can be put on display in classrooms, the library and the foyer. Bound collections of children's poetry and prose should sit in pride of place next to the school prospectus to be browsed by visitors.
- Send work to the local press and radio stations, especially if it can be linked to some special event.
- Invite parents in for celebration days.
- Involve parents in writing days during which they join in writing workshops alongside the children. Can we get a novelist, poet or illustrator along to help the event go with a bang? In my experience an author visit raises the profile of books for months to come.

Teachers can make a difference. We can help make a weak writer a little bit better, though don't expect miracles. We can certainly encourage average writers to improve and good ones to become very good ones. One thing we can't do is make great writers. If I knew how to do that I would be one! Great writing takes the sprinkle of fairy dust whose alchemy nobody has been able to analyse. In this book I am trying to provide a handbook which is both practical and theoretical. I want to help teachers and children develop a learning environment in which writing can flourish. I am not presumptuous enough to tell anyone how to write. The best writing comes through a process of reading, reflection and revision. Oh, and sometimes rebellion. Within the confines of most lessons we do little more than explore the mechanics of particular genres, but that is worthwhile in itself. What I am doing is passing on a few tips which work for me and might work for you.

Write on!

Alan Gibbons, September 2004

What makes a good writing lesson?

Story telling

People, when you come right down to it, are big bags of stories. We regale each other with our experiences and memories, our hopes, our dreams, our worries, our aspirations. We summon up the words and shape them into patterns. We make choices. Some words and phrases we add, some we delete. That is the nature of story-telling. At best it can take the reader by the hand and make her feel she was there, living the moments the writer describes. Story-telling should be at the very heart of learning in any good school. Many adults will, like me, go misty-eyed at the memory of sitting in a room with the sunlight on their face and the dust motes hanging in the slanting beams, listening to a loved story.

How short-sighted, then, for some schools to jettison story-time in the spurious pursuit of more time to 'get through' the curriculum. This is the notion of education as somebody with a pedagogical jug filling cups. Story-time, an oasis of quiet and respect for the cadences of language, is a seminal experience in many children's lives. It should be valued as such.

I met a strapping eighteen year old the other day who reminded me of the afternoons when he was six and I used Wolfie the glove puppet to entertain him and his class. Any teacher can become an accomplished story teller. Practice in this area, as in any human activity, makes, if not perfect, certainly better.

Here are some tips. To begin with, watch a good story-teller in action. Do they read in an unrelieved monotone or do they use inflection, changes of pace and voice? Watch their facial expressions, the way they move their hands, the way they catch the eyes of various members of their audience. If you read a story in a pedestrian drone or mumble into your chest don't be surprised if you lose your audience. If you are working with young children, why not use finger or hand puppets, or possibly magnetic characters on a felt board. In my first years as an infant teacher I had that fondly remembered story-telling puppet called Wolfie and, for maths, a particularly cute panda by the name of Sum Sum. Put some effort into it, some humour, some *joy*, and you will get a response.

It is good to start with the familiar.

Here is one example of an updated traditional tale:

Snow White and the Seven Dwarves

Once upon a time there was a lovely young princess called Snow White. She was loved by everyone, especially the birds and animals who came to the palace garden to listen to her sing her favourite chart-topping song, 'Someday my prince will come'.

Unfortunately, not everyone loved Snow White. Her nasty stepmother the Queen was so jealous of the beautiful young princess. Her skin would actually turn green with envy. Evening after evening she would go into the bathroom and consult the magic mirror which hung above the toilet.

'Mirror, mirror, in the lav,' she would say, 'who's the most beautiful you can have?'

'Not you, chuck,' the mirror would answer. 'Compared to Snow White you're like the back of a bus.'

Now the Queen knew the palace disco was approaching fast and she wanted to be the belle of the ball. She decided to get rid of Snow White. She called in Charlie the Woodcutter.

'Charlie,' she said, 'I want you to take Snow White into the woods and chop off her head.'

Charlie protested loudly.

'She's a lovely child,' he said. 'Why would I do her harm?'

'Because,' the Queen replied, 'if you don't I'll chop up your children for firewood.'

So, with a heavy heart, Charlie took Snow White into the woods for a picnic.

'Come on, Snowy girl,' he said.

Well, Snow White was just munching her way through her second sausage roll when Charlie sneaked behind her and pulled out his axe.

'Look out, look out,' called a passing bird. 'He's got an axe.'

Charlie hid the incriminating axe behind his back.

'Oh no, I haven't,' he said.

'Oh yes, you have,' said the bird.

'Oh no, I haven't.'

'Oh yes, you have.'

Refusing to believe Charlie could do anything so wicked, Snow White turned round and started to eat a doughnut. Once again Charlie whipped out his axe.

'Look out, look out,' called a passing rabbit. 'He's got an axe.'

Charlie once more hid the axe.

'Oh no, I haven't,' he said.

'Oh yes, you have,' the rabbit said.

'Oh no, I haven't.'

'Oh yes, you have.'

This time the bunny hopped over and tugged furiously until he pulled the axe out of Charlie's hand.

'See,' the bunny said. 'He's banged to rights.'

'Oh Charlie,' Snow White said. 'How could you?'

'I'm so sorry,' Charlie the Woodcutter sobbed. 'The wicked Queen made me do it.'

Snow White listened to Charlie's story and forgave him. To fool the Queen she smeared the axe with tomato ketchup.

'Show the Queen the axe covered with ketchup and she will think it is my blood,' Snow White told him. 'I'll find somewhere to hide.'

So Charlie showed the Queen the axe. She was delighted and started to try on new outfits for the palace disco. Meanwhile Snow White wandered through the woods and found a little cottage with seven little beds inside. The names on the beds were: Hunky, Dunky, Mr Funky, Clunky, Punky, Little Monkey and last of all Bob. Snow White lay down and fell asleep.

Meanwhile, down at the jam butty mines the seven dwarves were knocking off work.

'Hi ho,' they sang. 'Hi ho, hi ho, it's off to home we go, with a diddle-diddle-dee and a diddle-diddle-dee. Hi ho, hi ho, hi ho.'

When they got home they discovered Snow White fast asleep. She woke up and begged them for help. So they let her stay. But back at the palace the Queen was standing in front of the mirror over the toilet in her disco clothes.

'Mirror mirror in the lav,' she said. 'Now who's the most beautiful you can have?'

'Still not you, chuck,' said the mirror. 'Snow White remains the most beautiful in the land.'

'She lives!' cried the Queen. 'We'll see about that.'

Next day she disguised herself as an old lady and went to find the dwarves' cottage. When Snow White opened the door the old lady offered her a poisoned Mars Bar. Snow White took a bite and fell senseless to the floor.

Over at the jam butty mines the seven dwarves were knocking off work.

'Hi ho,' they sang. 'Hi ho, hi ho, it's off to home we go, with a diddle-diddle-dee and a diddle-diddle-dee. Hi ho, hi ho, hi ho.'

But when they got home they found Snow White senseless on the floor.

'She's dead,' the dwarves cried in despair, 'dead, dead, dead.'

But Bob, who was a medical student in his spare time, said: 'She's not dead. She's under a spell. Get the most handsome prince in the land to give her a big, sloppy kiss and she will be right as rain.'

So the seven dwarves set off across the kingdom on their motor bikes. Eventually, it was Little Monkey who found the most handsome prince in the kingdom, one Prince Ronan of Keating. He returned with Little Monkey and kissed Snow White better. She looked into his eyes and sang, 'This day my prince has come.'

So they lived happily ever after. Not so the wicked Queen. Halfway through the disco there was a puff of smoke. She turned into a little black beetle. She scurried away and was never seen again.

This updated fairy tale is a good example of a story which is always a winner with young children. It employs their previous knowledge and uses repeated patterns. It draws on TV, film and pop music and has lots of familiar elements. It also exploits the features of pantomime. There is plenty of room for funny voices and actions and it employs mischievous humour by subverting the conventions of the traditional tale. Weaving in local accents and place names always goes down well. With a little practice in front of the mirror most teachers can tell this sort of tale, or use elements of this sort of story-telling when reading a book. Teaching is performance. With a little investment in effort by the teacher, story-time can be made special and enriching, if not downright magical. Try telling other stories in the same vein. Jack and the Beanstalk can become a tale of a kindly old man with a glandular problem tormented by a naughty little thief called Jack. Hansel and Gretel can become the story of a kindly pensioner harassed by two spoilt brats from up the road. The possibilities are endless.

If you want to involve the children themselves have a story circle. Have a magic hat, as elaborate and eye-catching as possible, something the children would love to put on. Tell a familiar story in a chain. Each child tells part of the story then passes on the hat. You can only tell the next part of the story if you wear the hat. There are many variations on this theme. I have employed a karaoke microphone, a cardboard TV the child puts over his head and a story giant's chair.

If teachers and librarians have embedded a love of story-telling and books in the young writer, then that youngster will have a wonderful reservoir of literature from which to draw.

The child as author

There should be time in school for free writing. Young people should sometimes be permitted time to settle down and write whatever they like, in any style or genre they like, for as long as they like. Not everything in education has to be prescribed by the teacher. Many children can and do learn by themselves. They should be given space to do just that. Most writing in school will however take place in the classroom, and will be expected to be delivered within a set time. This isn't how most writers would choose to work, but it is something we have all been through and good writing can certainly be done in this context. Furthermore, much free, self-generated writing draws upon good models fostered previously in directed activities.

We can make several points about the child as author:

You learn to write by writing. It is like riding a bike. Theorising about the bike, drawing diagrams of it and studying its aero-dynamics might help, but nothing beats hoisting yourself up on that seat. Putting children's work onto OHP transparencies and demonstrating with a coloured OHP pen can demonstrate revision without putting the child through the laborious effort of re-drafting their own work. Pop in a subordinate clause to demonstrate more complex sentences, for example. Seeing it inserted in purple pen is more effective than a dozen worksheets. Endless re-drafting kills the child's pleasure in writing. A little judicious guidance with the young writer looking, listening and discussing can be tremendously valuable.

You learn the tricks of the trade by watching how other people write. The teacher should model a piece of writing in front of the children. It doesn't have to be the greatest piece of composition in the world. Once a month write the text of the day yourself. It will meet all your objectives, it will show the children you practise what you preach and finally it might just be fun. Many teachers baulk at this but, if we are asking children to write we should be prepared to do it ourselves.

You learn to write by imitating good practice and by receiving guidance. Be practical. You can't help every child, every lesson. Target a small group and intervene throughout the lesson. In the plenary session, draw on the work they have done to demonstrate the lesson objectives. Focusing on the children's work is the way to make the best of this part of the lesson. After all, there is only so much you can say about your objectives.

You need to absorb tricks and skills. The young David Beckham learned how to put spin on the ball, to bend it, to hit it with pace and power. The young writer also needs to learn skills. Like the young Becks, however, he needs to integrate all those skills into practice. In Beckham's case that is a competitive match. In the young writer's case it is a story.

You learn at least as much by the things you do wrong as the things you do right. Mistakes are not terminal. They are the reason for re-drafting. Crossing out is fine. After all, Shakespeare did it. Just look at the drafts of his plays. No marks for presentation there!

Now, how do we get started? A focus is needed, an enriched experience which acts as a stimulus. This can be a book the class has read, an interesting artefact, a piece of TV or film, some music, drama or artwork, an oral recollection, anything that provokes a response. Many youngsters are not verbal or oral learners. The expansive, kinaesthetic learner will appreciate drama as a bridge to writing. The visual learner will benefit from maps or diagrams. Brainstorming is an important technique which helps words and ideas come tumbling out and provides a resource to offer security and support.

The teacher as a walking writing frame

There is a vogue for writing frames. They can be useful in organising the young writer's ideas into a structure. They are however, in the last analysis, worksheets, and worksheets are *things*. They don't actually do anything. What really works is to see the teacher herself as a walking writing frame. She sets each short term objective. She defines the parameters of each section. She marshalls the writers' ideas and helps give a shape and a structure to them. She is the more experienced writer who sets the less experienced writer an example.

I use a basic four-part structure for these lessons:

The four part structure

1: Exposition/setting/opening. Here the writer sets out the mood, the genre, the main initial characters.

In this section the teacher should spend a lot of time setting out the ground rules. You need to get the reader's attention. The effect you are after is this: two hands come out of the pages of the book and grab your eyeballs. A striking opening sentence helps. Then, if a major objective is to pace the story and stop the young writer racing prematurely towards the end, the teacher has to model the kind of tension-building techniques which work.

2: Complication/problem. Here the writer introduces the obstacle the protagonist must overcome, the situation or dilemma in which they find themselves, which takes forward the plot and develops the story.

The teacher should break down the story in advance. She can then model the writing of the next episode in the story. Many children will not readily distinguish the different stages in the story. This has to be demonstrated or modelled.

3: Crisis/action. The main events of the story. Here, the main priority is to avoid crudeness. You need to make the reader see, hear, feel the experiences the main character undergoes. Break action down into slow motion. Look at Oliver Stone's movie *Platoon*. When the sergeant, played by William Dafoe, is gunned down by the Vietnamese army it isn't a matter of bang, you're dead. The bullet thumps into his back. His arms fly up in an image of crucifixion. His face contorts in agony. He slumps forward onto his knees. Finally he crashes face down on the earth. Examples such as this reinforce the writer's principle: show, don't tell. Again, stop the class and show how this can be done.

4: Resolution/ending. The way the story turns out. The teacher can, from her own reading and viewing, collect a range of endings which the children can employ in their own writing. The more you read, the more you understand the mechanics of narrative. The more you understand the mechanics of narrative, the better you can pass them on to your pupils. In fact, one useful literacy activity is to collect good opening lines from a selection of fiction. Have top tens of good openings. Then do the same with endings. It all helps focus the young writer on the process.

Just one technical point before we move on. I have watched many writing lessons and been appalled by the materials available to the teacher. A worn, scratchy blackboard hardly sends out the right message, does it? It helps the young writer enormously to see writing demonstrated on a good quality whiteboard or even an interactive screen. If the different clauses or parts of speech are displayed in different colours or fonts it helps the more visual learners to make sense of this odd process we call writing. Furthermore, there should be several surfaces on which to demonstrate the various aspects of the writing process. On one the teacher can model the text. On another, sample sentence starters, connectives and useful vocabulary can be displayed. A third can be provided for differentiation, either for the more able or for the less able. Finally, the children should have access to individual whiteboards to draft sentences or try out spellings.

The trouble with boys

The problem

In the introduction of this book I quoted the findings of a recent Ofsted report that about half of all boys start secondary school without having achieved the average Level 4 standard in writing. More recently Ofsted has indicated a seventeen percentage point gap between boys' and girls' attainment. Another disturbing statistic is this: boys are four times more likely to be labelled as emotionally and behaviourally disturbed than girls. They are similarly far more likely to be excluded from school. The gender gap appears to be big and growing. As a result there has been much gnashing of teeth and wringing of hands about this problem of male underachievement.

It is important to get the problem in perspective. Not so long ago there was a similar panic about girls' under-achievement. We should be wary of 'fads', of throwing the baby out with the bathwater. There remains a large minority of girls who similarly under-achieve. Their needs should not be forgotten in the drive to help the boys.

Some of the problems teachers encounter with boys are perennial. Some appear to be of more recent vintage. The perennial problems include the following:
- Boys often have different learning styles (auditory, visual, kinaesthetic) which have not been easily accommodated by sedentary, academic, verbally-based teaching approaches.
- Boys tend to be more impulsive than girls.
- Boys often feel they can succeed without working. They need disproportionately more explanation, encouragement and reward than girls.
- Boys need immediate satisfaction and approval.
- Boys do not readily see the point of activities. It is vital that lessons are purposeful and relevant.
- Boys mature later – literacy/vocabulary development can lag behind.
- Boys tend to have stronger visual/spatial/technical intelligences.
- Boys are often weaker with work involving empathy, metaphor, figurative language.

None of this however explains the recent *widening* of the gap between boys' and girls' attainment. All those traditional features of male behaviour seem to have been accentuated by social changes. Child poverty is arguably the single greatest determinant of educational achievement. Seen in that context, here is a key statistic. Between 1979 and 1993 the number of men earning below the European decency threshold doubled from 14.6% to 29.3%. It is worth keeping in mind, of course, that the figure for women is around 50%! The point is, however, that the relative decline in male manual earning power and employment has had a disproportionate effect on male self-esteem. In some areas women have become the main wage-earner. Whether we like it or not, this has had a significant impact on men's self-esteem. With the decline of male manual employment in many areas, large numbers of boys do not 'see the point' of education, believing, not without cause, that they will have limited employment opportunities when they leave school. Unable to achieve status through the job market, many boys seek it in anti-social behaviour and crime, earning credibility for being cock of the gang, for being 'hard.'

Alternatives to the attraction of the street have shrunk. There are far fewer apprenticeships, for example, and the social importance of apprenticeships for adolescent males can't be over-stressed. It was never been simply a matter of learning a trade. Apprenticeship definitely had an important socialising effect. There is a strong case that it is not boys *per se* who underachieve, but that it is disproportionately working class boys who do so. From this point of view, issues of gender are refracted through those of social class.

If you agree even partly with this explanation, it is easy to see how the world of education can be problematic for boys. Men are under-represented in education, especially in early years and junior education. Boys don't see themselves reflected in the world of school. It can appear to be a feminine environment. I have been in many primary schools where there have been only one or two male teachers. Sometimes there are none at all. This is clearly a problem, and school staffing should be much more balanced than it is. This is not to say female teachers can't provide excellent role models for our boys. Many of us learned principally from our mothers, after all. The problem remains however that large numbers of boys do not see their own masculinity reflected in school. In the long term it is vital that more men are attracted to early years and junior education to create a more balanced environment. A sexist educational pyramid composed of predominantly female early years teachers at the bottom and mainly male managers and policy-makers at the top is helpful to nobody.

We can further point to a number of possible reasons why boys underachieve in writing. Creativity and competition can be stifled by a rigid curriculum. A curriculum based upon prescription and testing tends to antagonise the underachieving boys we highlighted above, making them alienated or even rebellious. Teacher perception can also be a problem. In the last week of August one year a colleague was preparing her classroom. She had a 'naughty boys' table. I pointed out that she hadn't met the children yet so how did she know there would be any naughty boys? Her reply? 'Mr Gibbons, the naughty boy is always with us.'

Finally, there is little question that a significant – and unwelcome – anti-swot culture has developed in many schools. 'Streetwise' and macho posturing might be seen as a partial attempt to compensate for the lack of male self-esteem on offer in the job market to the less academic of our boys. Reading for pleasure, enthusiasm in class and academic success attract disapproval at best and bullying at worst. I have encountered many youngsters on my travels who help out in the school library at lunchtime as a sanctuary from what can be a tough world outside.

This demands a major counter-offensive. Figures from the world of sport, business and culture should be employed to demonstrate that success is something to be aspired to and that a good education is an indispensable factor in that success. More importantly, teaching strategies have to take into account the male behaviours described above. Failure to do so would mean accepting in the long term a tail of male under-achievement.

There seem to me to be three elements to this approach:
- Recognise perennial boys' behaviour, and employ teaching strategies best suited to it.
- Recognise the difficulties produced by social changes, and take measures to counteract their effects.
- Resist any temptation to pander to the negative attitudes (sexism, aggression, macho street culture) social changes produce.

Reading

We can often compound the problem by not recognising the kinds of books boys will enjoy. I was once standing with a Head of English in a good comprehensive school. A Year 8 boy walked past carrying Stephen King's *The Stand*, a whopper of a book running to over 1,000 pages.

'That,' the teacher opined, 'is one of our non readers.'

When I asked him to explain that astonishing observation he told me, 'Well, it isn't literature. It's just horror, isn't it?'

'Yes,' I replied, 'Like *King Lear* is just horror. Remember Lear having his eyes ripped from his head? *Out vile jelly*. Then what about the witches' scene from *Macbeth*? Can you imagine anything more horrific for the average man than a woman with a beard?'

I could have gone on. In fact, I probably did, asking him if he remembered Mary Shelley's *Frankenstein*, Emily Bronte's *Wuthering Heights*, Charlotte Bronte's *Jane Eyre* or the work of Edgar Allen Poe. Can anyone seriously argue that horror isn't a key element of this literature?

The point is that there is still a literary snobbery about the subjects that many, though not all, boys enjoy. Some adults just can't accept that horror, adventure, graphic novels, sport or comics are suitable reading material. They just aren't literary enough. Well, I'd argue that you are more likely to get a boy reading John Le Carré or James Ellroy in the future if he is experiencing Anthony Horowitz now. He is more likely to pick up Bram Stoker or Ann Rice if he has read Darren Shan. He is more likely to savour Tolkien if he has encountered Eoin Colfer. Besides, Horowitz, Shan and Colfer are terrific authors in their own right. They are keeping a generation of boys reading.

We need to look at what boys are reading and help them find other books in the same vein that they might enjoy. If necessary, we have to begin with accessible, short reads such as the Barrington Stoke or Heinemann High Impact series. There is now a wide range of excellent material for less able readers. As we get boys reading we have to keep faith with them and not impose arbitrary standards of what is literature. Legitimate boy-friendly genres should not be neglected in favour of snobbery. Giving a child no book is bad. Giving them the wrong book could well be worse. The notion that if it isn't dull or worthy, it isn't literature should be consigned to the dustbin, and the sooner the better. There is no better way to stop boys writing well than by killing their interest in reading through toe-curlingly mistaken notions of what is literary.

The lesson

The scaffolding approach works particularly well for boys. It appeals to those lads who have visual or kinaesthetic approaches to learning. The teacher breaks down the lesson into bite-sized segments. By this method he is offering the boys short term, realisable objectives. They know what is expected of them and can be given a time-limited target if necessary. ('Three or four sentences of really gory description in five minutes, please.') This appeals to that large proportion of boys (again, by no means all) who crave immediate feedback, approval and advice.

Colleagues working for the National Literacy Strategy in Cumbria recently undertook an informal survey of what works with boys. Their conclusion? That it was in the schools that had fast-paced, well-structured lessons, laced with humour, that the gap between boys' and girls' achievement was the narrowest. The survey is neither large-scale nor scientific but the conclusions seem extremely plausible.

A good balance of girl- and boy-friendly subjects for writing is essential. It keeps both groups engaged. Diagrams labelled with useful vocabulary helps support the children, forming a resource they can consult. Of course, a balance of subject matter also addresses the fact that there are many boys who like more sensitive, contemplative subject matter and many girls who like adventure and horror. We should be careful not to shoehorn our children into rigid gender stereotypes. There is a wide spectrum of behaviours and we should encourage respect for all of them and adapt our teaching according to the children's needs.

So what am I saying? Basically, it boils down to this. There is a problem of boys' under-achievement in writing. We should not exclude any genre which might capture their imagination on the spurious grounds that it is un-literary. Purposeful, confident scaffolded teaching works so long as it isn't the only method employed. Many boys do not fit the standard impulsive image. Schools should accommodate all learning styles. We can make a difference on three conditions:

- Boys need good quality books which appeal to them and not just to the teacher's preconception of what they need.
- Boys need lessons which match their style of learning.
- The interests of boys should be addressed without neglecting the girls.

A model lesson

Ghost story

You are onto a winner with a ghost story. Unfortunately, many of our pupils think a ghost story goes something like this:

Once upon a time there was a ghost. I chopped his head off and then I kicked him and then I biffed him and then I threw his body in the yard. Then I went home for my tea, then I realised it was all a dream. The end.

This is a piece of caricature but it encapsulates all that is wrong in some young people's writing. It relies almost exclusively on straightforward chronological organisation ('… and then …'). It also has a routine opening and an ineffective ending. Why? Well, this child doesn't read, does he?

OK, let's start the lesson with the principle I outlined above: good quality speaking and listening precedes good quality reading and writing. So let's encourage a lively discussion of the task ahead. The child who knows what he is doing is more likely to produce good work.

The child is going to write a first person narrative about exploring a haunted house one night. He can select his own ghost/vampire/demon. The point is: he should not give away what it is. He keeps it locked away in a metaphorical steel safe in his head. I once actually had a safe on my classroom wall, made out of a cornflake box painted silver. I would physically place inside it the vocabulary and features I wanted the children to delay introducing in order to build tension. Sometimes graphic display is worth hours of nagging!

To build tension effectively, therefore, he will not introduce the creature until later. In fact he should also hide the house, concealed as it is by the trees. He can give a glimpse of its outline if he wants, but he is to keep the reader in suspense. This is Chris Tarrant tension-building: 'Have you won a million? We'll tell you after this break!' I usually set no more than two short term objectives for paragraph one. These are:
• Show, don't tell
• Build tension.

An anecdote helps clarify what we are about to the class:

Take a movie like Jurassic Park. The plot is simple. It pretty much boils down to this:
• *Four people arrive on a tropical island.*
• *They get chased by a big dinosaur – grr!*
• *They run away..*
• *They hide in a kitchen and get chased by some small dinosaurs – grr!*

- *They run away.*
- *They end up in a room with a big dinosaur and a small dinosaur.*
- *The big dinosaur eats the small dinosaur.*
- *The people escape in a helicopter – hurrah!*

What brings the film to life is the way the story unfolds. Remember how we meet the Tyrannosaurus Rex. A glass of water trembles. Something wicked this way comes. Trees thresh about. Something big and wicked this way comes. We see the rope to which the goat was tied. No goat now. The rope is bloodstained. Something big, wicked and very hungry this way comes. Then it eats the man on the lavatory. Release of tension!

This demonstrates the two short-term objectives. The images of the glass of water, the trees, the rope, give clues about the creature which is about to appear. Furthermore, we don't get to see the star of the show, the Tyrannosaurus Rex, until the story-teller, Stephen Spielberg, has built the tension by dropping lots of clues.

At this point I introduce a map (Figure 3). I set out the *geography* of the narrative, if you will. This helps those visual learners in our schools because they can actually see what we mean. It is there, concretely in front of them. What is the role of the forest, for example? Is it there because the writer likes vegetation? Of course not. It is there to hide the haunted house, to build the tension. I then ask the children for ideas. What would they see and hear if they, as the main character, were walking through the woods? The teacher should then scribe some of the best ideas on a whiteboard for the class to use as a resource:

<u>*I heard*</u>
the wheezing/sighing/whistling of the wind
the creaking of the branches
footsteps
twigs snapping
leaves or gravel crunching underfoot
the roll of thunder in the distance
the thud of raindrops
the hiss of rain on the forest floor
the thud of your own heartbeat
the catch of your own breath

Ghost Story

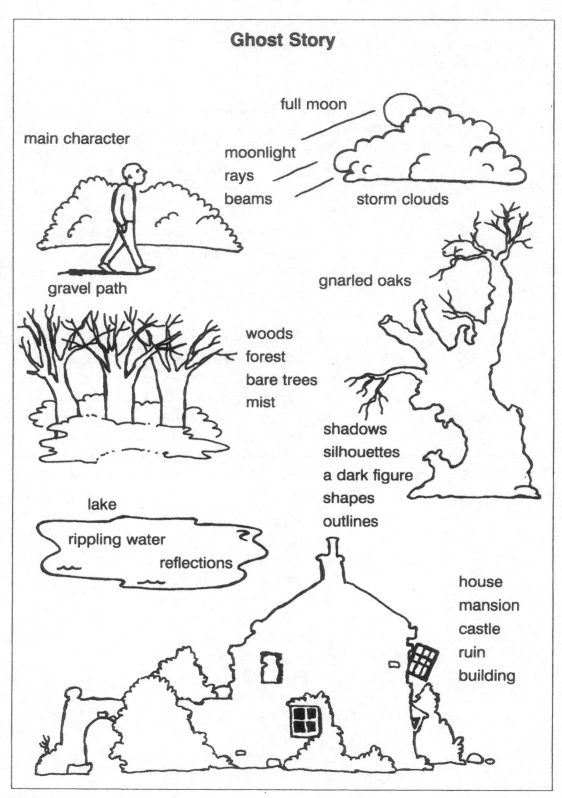

main character

full moon

moonlight
rays
beams

storm clouds

gravel path

gnarled oaks

woods
forest
bare trees
mist

shadows
silhouettes
a dark figure
shapes
outlines

lake

rippling water

reflections

house
mansion
castle
ruin
building

Figure 3

This list is far from exhaustive. The teacher's job is then to show how you can turn these ideas into effective imagery:
- a simile – *twigs snapped like broken bones underfoot*
- a metaphor – *the wind wheezed and sighed, a broken, old man labouring through the woods*

I saw
a dark figure
a silhouette
a shape
an outline
the bare branches of the trees
lightning shimmering on the horizon
mist rolling through the woods
the darkness
the murk
the blackness
the gloom
the storm clouds
the moonlight

Again the teacher can demonstrate how to use these ideas to create telling imagery:
- a simile – *the mist was like a silvery curtain threaded between the trees*
- a metaphor – *the night was a gauntlet clinging to my face*

It is also worth demonstrating other, more interesting, ways of saying *I saw* or *I heard*:
- *Out of the corner of my eye, I glimpsed …*
- *The night air filled with the sounds of …*
- *Something crossed my vision …*
- *A sound filtered through the darkness.*

Now, before we actually get into telling the reader what the protagonist saw and heard on her walk through the woods, what about the opening line? Let's face it, 'One day' or 'Once upon a time' doesn't really cut it any more.

Try something like this:
- *It was midnight, the dead of night, out in the woods.*
- *From the moment I entered the woods I knew I wasn't alone.*

There you go, in the first example you are actually teaching subordinate clauses in context! As mentioned above, a good activity is to collect story openings (and endings) in a notebook, or display them around the classroom.

OK, we've got our writers to think about their opening line. Now let's get started. To begin the story the child can enjoy exploring how to build an atmosphere of suspense and fear. The teacher's job then becomes one of asking questions and suggesting vocabulary:

- What did the moon look like? *A milky eye stared blindly.*
- What colour were the storm clouds? Could you combine more than one adjective for effect? *Inky blue-black storm clouds rolled across the face of the moon.*
- Give me a strong verb for the way the darkness crept through the woods? *Fingers of darkness scrabbled between the trees.*

This is teaching, using your professional judgement to advise, assist, demonstrate, encourage. Teaching is also the professional judgement you make as to *how much* you prescribe, to what extent you direct, advise. Somehow you must balance the desire to teach structure and the need to give children the space to take their story in their own directions. And where does the language come from that the teacher is using? Why, from their own reading, of course! It is in your Stephen King, your Dean Koontz, your Shirley L. Jackson, your M.R James or Susan Hill, so dig it out.

When the children are underway, ask them to think about weaving in other elements. How did they feel? Don't just say *I was scared* or *I was petrified*. That is telling, not showing and it doesn't scare anybody. Try this sort of thing instead:

- *Fear trickled down my spine.*
- *Anxiety crept over my flesh.*
- *The hairs on the back of my neck stood up like needles.*
- *My blood turned to ice.*

Could they use internal monologue? Try:

- *Was there something out there or was I imagining it?*
- *Was that the wind whining or was it the sound of an unnamed creature stalking me?*

Finally, show some ways a paragraph could end:

- *Then the darkness was inside me. It was like a cockroach burrowing through my brain.*
- *I was drowning in an ocean of fear.*

The results can be pretty purple, but let's face it, our problem is not children over-writing! It is mechanical, impoverished prose from which we often suffer. We can always show them how to trim things back and make it more economical when they are older and more mature as writers. It is easier, in the teenage years, to trim back over-writing than to enrich threadbare writing.

Paragraph Two could start with the protagonist at last seeing the house/ruin/castle. Here the teacher can set a new short-term objective. Describe the haunted house as if it were a living creature. This is the technique of personification. I usually stop the writers, stressing that they should not feel rushed and should take as long as they wish to explore the mood in Paragraph One. You know you are winning when they ask to finish it for homework! I suggest a linking or transitional sentence, for example:

- *That's when I saw the house.*
- *The house came into view and my heart stuttered.*

The whole of this paragraph should then be a detailed, evocative description of this key character, the house itself. It helps to brainstorm this section before proceeding.

The house
windows like empty eye sockets
a door like a withered mouth
brickwork like a scarred face
guttering creaking in the wind
crouching gargoyles
roofs slick with rain
yellowish candlelight in the window

The point is to stimulate the children's imagination, to enable them to write with texture.

My inclination now would be to conclude the lesson and return to it another day. This avoids the 'dribble away' factor. I always stress to the children that no professional writer completes a whole story in one go. We re-read it. We think about it. Sometimes we even dream about it. We mull it over or get somebody else to read it and give their opinion. That is good practice. Writing is not done in a vacuum. It takes two to participate in this particular tango: the writer and her oft-forgotten familiar, the reader. Maybe two children could act as writing buddies, commenting constructively (this takes training!) on one another's work. To foster this kind of attention to one's work, the teacher could choose a couple of good examples and make overhead projector transparencies of them. Praising the children's work, they could sensitively indicate one or two areas where redrafting might help improve it, and make a good piece of work even better. Remember: redrafting is adding or deleting text to improve the story, not tidying up spelling or handwriting!

In my opinion this is all that is needed. Forever asking children to redraft makes them bored and kills their enthusiasm and creativity. So long as they develop an understanding of what they can do to improve their work they do not need to be forever working and re-working the text. Had I been asked to do that back in Crewe Grammar School for Boys I might never have become a professional writer. The dream would have died of boredom.

When the teacher returns to this story, he should encourage the children to re-read their work before they put pen to paper. This is what a 'real' writer does, reading chapter ten before embarking on chapter eleven. He does it for continuity, so that he resumes from where he left off. Furthermore, it achieves a consistency of tone. Now we are ready to discuss the issues involved in the action of the story. What is paramount here is avoiding the dreadful crime of: *And then … and then … and then …*. Some schools try to do this by fetishising lists of connectives and conjunctions. To be honest, it isn't that much of an improvement to read a story which goes: *And then … next … after that … finally.* It is still plodding and routine. A better way is to study and teach the various sentence structures good writers use. Try:

- A clause to open the sentence: *Heart thudding, I inched forward.*
- Direction phrases: *All around me the forest was coming alive.* Or: *Something moved in the distance, a blurry form.*
- Repetition: *With each step, with each laboured breath, I moved forward.*

Just as we mapped the geography of the woods, we should now map the geography of the house's interior. Once more we could brainstorm ideas:

Inside the house
staircases
banisters
stained glass windows
floorboards
timbers
ceilings
chandeliers
mirrors
portraits
radiators
panels
passages
corridors

As before, the teacher could initiate a discussion. How do we bring the house alive?
- *The radiators thumped as if a heart was beating away inside them.*
- *Uncertain images floated in the mirrors.*
- *The stained glass windows cast a crimson light throughout the house.*

This section of the story is more or less a walk from the front door to the room where evil is waiting for you. We have structured the story to demonstrate pace.

We can now give the children a lot of freedom, a choice of pathways. It is not the teacher's job to decide what happens in the story, but to facilitate the child's telling of it. Let them ask you: 'Can I go in this direction?' If you think it will kill the story, say because they want to detonate an atomic bomb (the vampire will no longer exist, but neither will the whole of Merseyside!), suggest two or three other pathways which might offer better, less drastic, solutions. To this aim, always brainstorm the alternatives so they do not slip into, yes, you guessed it: *And then … and then … and then.*

The pupils can be reminded that they should have an idea of their ghost or monster in their head. This will determine what clues they give the reader:

- Is the house itself the evil? If so, it might be coming to life around you, speaking to you inside your mind.
- Is there a ghost waiting for you? If so, you could discover an old book, a yellowed newspaper, a portrait. A ghost story is usually a tale of unfinished business. Also, is the ghost evil or just a tormented, misunderstood spirit craving justice? It will affect the way the writer concludes the story.
- Is it a vampire? If so, you might see bats or hear hissing.
- Is it a demon, a creature drawn completely from your own imagination? If so, give it a name, one that suggests its character maybe. Describe its appearance, its nature.

This is planting elements of the resolution within the body of the story. Remember *Jaws*. The shark dies because Roy Schneider's character shoots the gas tank in the creature's mouth. But Stephen Spielberg has to show the gas tanks earlier in the movie or the whole thing is a cheap trick.

Finally, we come to the resolution. Here they should build on the clues they have dropped in the earlier parts of the story. Remind the children of the earlier principles:

- Show, don't tell
- Build tension.

So, don't say: '*Ooh, it's a vampire.*'

Do say: '*A heavy cloak slid on the floor. Frosty breath chilled the air. Dark eyes stared into my soul.*'

Endings can be broken down into two kinds: the closed ending and the open ending.

Closed ending – this is where all the loose ends are tied up.

- There could be a struggle and you destroy the creature.
- You could escape.

Open ending – this is where you leave the reader guessing.
- You think you have escaped but the creature returns. *Through the window pane I saw its fiery eyes staring at me. It seemed to say: I'm back!*
- By slipping from the past to the present tense you leave the reader with a chill. *I feel my resistance slipping away. I am under the spell of my dark master. I am lost.*

Here is an example of the finished product. This was written with an open ending.

The Haunting

By Emily Casey, Year 5

It was midnight, the dead of night in the forest.

I heard mysterious creatures howling in the distance. The wind was wheezing and groaning down my ears. I could hear footsteps, thudding like a fist. My heart was pounding.

My fear enveloped me like a glove clutching my face. I glanced around and saw a silhouette that was not there a moment ago.

A misty, silver curtain slid open like a velvet cloak and a black figure emerged.

I started to run. The night was creeping inside me. It was like a centipede rippling through my bones.

Then I saw the house. The brickwork was like crooked teeth laughing at me in the face. The windows were like empty eye sockets staring at me. The door was like a vortex drawing me in. I had no choice! I had to enter!

The feeling, it was like a black magnet taking me to a room, the cellar. But I was very surprised and shocked at what I saw.

I saw a sleek, black cat. I went down to stroke it but I knew I shouldn't, this urge inside me was forcing me. I bent down to stroke it and suddenly jumped back, it was evolving into something – it was a DRACULA!

I tried to run but the door shut and automatically locked itself. His fiery eyes were flaming like scarlet rubies. I grabbed a chair nearby and threw it at him with all my might. He stumbled to the ground.

I ran for the open window and all I heard was, "I'll be back!"

I was in my bed the next night, not daring to leave my room when I heard a slight tapping on my window. I drew back my curtains and he was there! He was back! I had no escape!

Lucky enough though, I had holy water in my bedroom from my uncle Matt's funeral.

"Sorry Uncle Matt!" I gasped under my breath, it's either this or DIE!

With all my might I lashed the holy water at him and in an instant he came up with red boils everywhere, but he still *wasn't dead*! This was some tough Dracula!

He was *still* clinging onto the window sill! I took my paper weight off my desk and bashed the tips of his fingers. He crashed to the ground at last!

"Curse you! Curse you!" he spluttered, "I promise I will be back! We will fight to the death!"

He staggered to the house of the previous event with fingers bleeding to the bone, a bad back and broken and chipped fingernails. Ha! He could scratch no more.

I watched him, he was about to turn the corner when he turned around for any sign of movement or any prying eyes when he turned into the sleek black cat again. He strolled around the corner and was gone in the blink of an eye.

Dawn was just approaching so I clambered into bed and I managed to get a few hours sleep before school.

That morning when I was in class, I nearly toppled off my chair. The principal, Mr Edges, entered our classsroom closely followed by DRAC!

"Good morning children," drawled Mr Edges.

"Good morning Mr Edges," chorused the children back to him.

"Now as you know, your ordinary teacher, Mrs Smith is very ill, so I have found you a very pleasant substitute, Mr Alucard," he drawled once more.

"Now I would like you to treat him with respect, just the same as me."

A murmur of laughter travelled around the room as quick as the blink of an eye.

"Now children, I'm serious!" snapped Mr Edges.

Then I realised it. Alucard is Dracula spelled backwards! He was out to get me and this time, I felt that he was going to be successful. Was this the end of Emily Casey?

As an extension, following the same pattern, older children could tell the story in the second person, addressing the reader directly. This story assumes that the reader is somehow in league with the evil in the house and the reader plays the part of their unwitting victim. In re-telling the story using a different voice you change the content. This is an example of progression. Here is an example:

Hill House

By Thomas Clarke, Year 8

It is midnight, the dead of night at Hill House. Follow me down the long avenue of trees. Can you hear the owls hooting and a dog barking from far off? And there, the wind wheezing like a dying man. Can you hear that? Is it small creatures in the bushes? Do you see the moon from behind the clouds and the trees that never sleep?

Round the corner you will see the house. Are you uneasy yet? Can you hear the creaking of doors and cracked window panes? Can you see the crumbled brickwork, a single light bulb shining?

Ready to go inside? Nervous yet? Can you see the banister all cracked and ready to fall? See the cobwebs hanging everywhere. Hear the creaking of the floorboards or the grandfather clock ticking.

Sorry, what did you say? You want to go! Already? We're at the heart of the house. You should go into the cellar where it's dark and damp. See the old driers and the old Victorian washing machines. See the old clothes, the ones that belonged to the dead. Can you feel breathing on your neck? Our journey's over now and you're on your own. I forgot to mention the monster that lives here. Goodbye, try to get out alive.

If you can!

Hopefully, we now have a story of some richness and quality. It has taken considerable investment in terms of time, effort, thought and preparation. But you only get out of something what you are prepared to put into it. While writing their final paragraph the young writer can be reminded that the last line should be as effective and resonant as the opening one. A class activity could be, as I said earlier, to collect favourite openings and endings in a class book. What adult will ever forget the first line of *Rebecca* or the telling concluding line of *Tess of the D'Urbervilles* when Hardy says the Gods 'had finished their sport with Tess'?

So, we can ask the young writer, what works best? The great thing is that few readers will agree. Their opinions are as diverse as they are.

As I said earlier, this is not a plan to be followed slavishly. It is a demonstration lesson, a way of getting teachers to think about the structure of the writing lesson, what works and what doesn't. To be successful, this approach makes several assumptions:

- The teacher reads
- The child reads
- Writing can be fun
- Less experienced writers learn from more experienced ones
- Scaffolding helps the young writer focus on immediately realisable objectives. It is an approach which works particularly well with boys.
- Good teaching begins with this axiom: minimise planning to maximise teaching. Sometimes, in recent years, you could have got the message that it might be better to do away with the children altogether. They just get in the way of planning!

There you go then. That is how I approach my writing lessons. Through similarly structured activities we can develop in our young people a repertoire of skills from which they can draw. Pedestrian writing comes from the cerebral cortex of your brain. Good writing wells up from your soul. It bubbles in the ventricles of your heart. It seeps from every fibre of your being. It is up to the children to use what they have read and what they have been taught to produce something different and new, something that is distinctively *theirs*.

PART 2

The Lessons

How this section works

In the following pages you will find a series of sample lessons. They work like this:

- There is a short lesson plan based loosely on the *Grammar for Writing* materials.
- There is sometimes an illustration which can be photocopied for pupil use.
- There is a sample of children's work, with comments.
- Finally, there are some suggestions for follow-up.

All these samples are taken from my own teaching. They were all completed within the standard fifty or sixty minute lesson. As a visiting author I rarely have the luxury of teaching a piece of writing over a sequence of lessons. The stories have not been re-drafted. They are reproduced as they were given to me at the end of the lesson. With Year 5 and 6 children and pupils in secondary schools I generally stuck to the four paragraph structure. With younger children I relaxed this to some extent. In line with the observations on redrafting made above, some pieces of work were reproduced on overhead projector transparencies later. Using an OHP pen the class teacher would demonstrate correction and redrafting of the original material.

I hope this section proves useful to a new generation of teachers.

The piece of writing is there to give the reader an idea of what they might expect as an end product. The story can stand alone, or be used as part of the process of future teaching. The decision is yours.

Lesson 1

A story of the walking dead

Working titles: *Night of the living dead,*
**   *Dead walkers***

Lesson Plan

Objective: to understand how tension is built through pace, silences and delivery.

Stimulus: discussion of horror movies.

Sentence level: short sentences, strong verbs, adjectives.

Shared writing: using techniques of tension in the opening paragraph.

Guided writing: continue the story, building on the opening.

Structure of the lesson

Paragraph 1 (opening)

Choose a good opening line: *It was coming from under the earth, a repetitive, insistent scratching.*

Writing in the first person, describe the graveyard, the deconsecrated church, boarded up and derelict. Describe the railings. Possibly drop hints, describing them like exposed ribs. Use mist, the moon, the weather, to build atmosphere. The description should focus on cues which are visual, auditory, visceral. Describe the narrator's mounting anxiety. (e.g. *anxiety rippled down my spine*)

Paragraph 2 (complication)

First describe just a single finger emerging from the earth. How does it move? Is it rotting? Can you see the tendons, the bone? Can you come up with a simile? (e.g. *a fat, slimy slug*)

Next describe a hand emerging? What is it like? What similes/metaphors can you use here?

Then show the head and shoulders, and finally the whole body erupting from beneath the earth. What is the face like? How does the soil burst around the creature's head and shoulder? End the chapter on the chilling moment when the zombie looks at you and thinks ... dinner!

Zombie Story

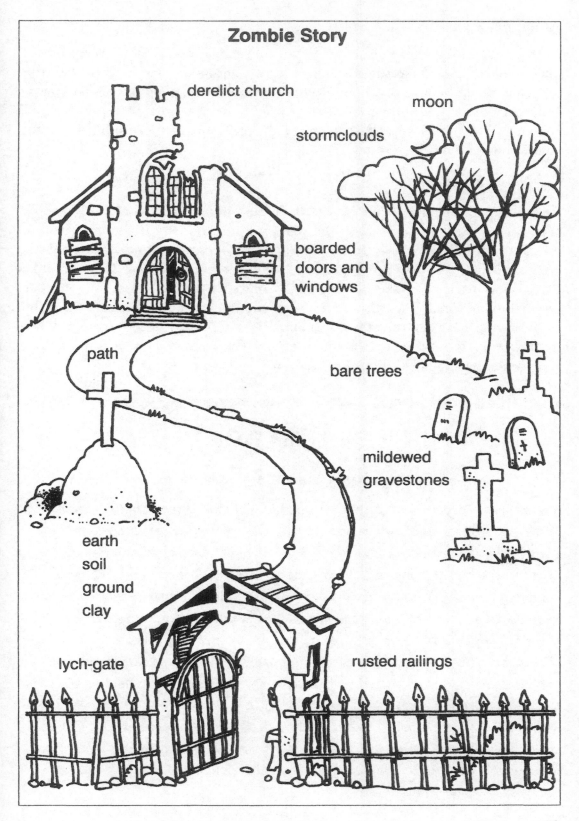

derelict church

moon

stormclouds

boarded doors and windows

path

bare trees

mildewed gravestones

earth
soil
ground
clay

lych-gate

rusted railings

Paragraph 3 (action)

Describe it coming after you. How does it move? Is it fast or slow? What makes it a zombie? Physical description makes the reader able to see it. How does the main character feel – revolted, disgusted? Use strong, figurative language. Consider internal monologue. Finally, where do you go to escape? Do you retreat into the church? How can you make the scene of the zombie attacking vivid? What details do you need?

Paragraph 4 (resolution)

Before putting pen to paper, look ahead to your ending. If dawn is going to come then slowly bring in mentions of the yellowing horizon, etc. If you are going to escape drop hints as to how. Build the possibility of escape into the action. If the creature is going to be destroyed, how? No tricks, or guns. Plant the germ of its destruction earlier in the narrative. A shard of broken glass might offer opportunities. Finally, if you want an open ending, do you escape then hear the creature approaching, relentless, unstoppable? Or could you shift from the past to the present tense and end with the narrator being dragged underground, their mouth filling with earth? The choice is yours.

Examples of children's work

The Living Dead

By Emily Hemsley, Year 8

Maybe the shortcut wasn't such a good idea. I looked around me. A thick mist was twirling and curling around the old, crumbly gravestones. The gate that I had left open creaked annoyingly. The mist started slowly rising, its cold fingers feeling here and there. Gravel crunched beneath my feet. A rumble, where did it come from? There it was again, a distinct tremor which seemed to come from under the earth. It seemed to go on for longer this time. I stopped dead in my tracks and that's when I saw it.

A blackened finger with veins coming out of the side was pulsing slowly. The bone stuck out of the end of its flesh. The fingernail was held on by one piece of blackened flesh.

I bent down to examine this finger for, although I was scared, I was also curious. It jumped. It grabbed hold of me. I opened my mouth to scream for now a whole hand had emerged from the soil. I couldn't scream! My mouth had frozen with fright.

The head, mouldy and missing one eye, burst through the soil. It was also missing the end of its nose and there were spaces in its rotting teeth. The maggots crawled around inside the skin that was left on its head. I screamed and the monster slowly turned its head and stared, now fully emerged from the earth.

I ran, afraid that this thing was going to take my life away from me. I stumbled and looked back. I should never have done that. I should never have come here. I ran into the church. The monster was slowly plodding up the hill. It banged on the doors and windows. I barricaded myself inside.

Then it stopped. Nothing. No noise. No tremors. No nothing. Then a sudden eruption, and there it was in the middle of the church.

Comments

This example comes from an older writer from Doncaster. It is powerfully written and evocative. It employs techniques of tension. It uses description to effect. It also displays an understanding of various sentence structures.

To follow up this work it might be a good idea to explore a similar suspenseful story in which there are two main characters. The objective here would be to examine how to show character. This would not be by over-burdening the reader with authorial information, but by drawing on ideas from the 'Show, Don't Tell' canon:

- Show character through the ways in which a character behaves. Do they act impulsively or nervously? Do they jump with fright? Is one more dominant?
- Show character through dialogue. How can we show character traits through the things they say to each other?

Another horror story could be, for instance, a mummy story in which the main character is the first explorer to open a long-forgotten tomb.

Paragraph 1: discovering the tomb. Describe it and your feelings.

Paragraph 2: the sarcophagus opens. Bit by bit, the mummy emerges.

Paragraph 3: the pursuit.

Paragraph 4: how is the creature defeated, returned to its sarcophagus?

Lesson 2

An upside-down fairy tale: Hansel and Gretel

Working title: *The little old lady and the two naughty children*

Lesson Plan

Objective: to produce a modern re-telling of a known traditional tale, using humour.

Stimulus: traditional telling of Hansel and Gretel or a modern re-telling such as *Hansel and Gretel* by Anthony Browne.

Sentence level: sentences and clauses. Setting out speech.

Shared writing: opening the story using devices from the traditional tale and a different viewpoint.

Guided writing: continue the tale inverting positive and negative characters.

Structure of the lesson

Introduction

Give a partial re-telling of the story. You only need the part about the witch's house:

Hungry and lost, Hansel and Gretel arrived at such an odd, little cottage in the woods. It was made of sweets and chocolate and gingerbread. Unable to contain themselves the children fell upon the walls and started eating. They were still chewing on the biscuit walls when a wicked witch appeared at the front door.

'Eat me out of house and home, will you?' she shrieked.

With that, she marched the children inside. Hansel she began to fatten up. Gretel she set to work doing the housework. Gretel soon realised what the witch was doing. She told Hansel that whenever the witch asked him to hold out his arm to see how he was fattening up he should hold out a chicken bone instead.

Day after day the witch tested Hansel's arm. Each time the little boy held out a chicken bone. The witch just couldn't understand why he wasn't getting fatter.

In the end she decided to eat him anyway. But as the witch dragged Hansel to

Witch Story

Inside:

adjectives:
comfy
soft
cosy
warm
bright

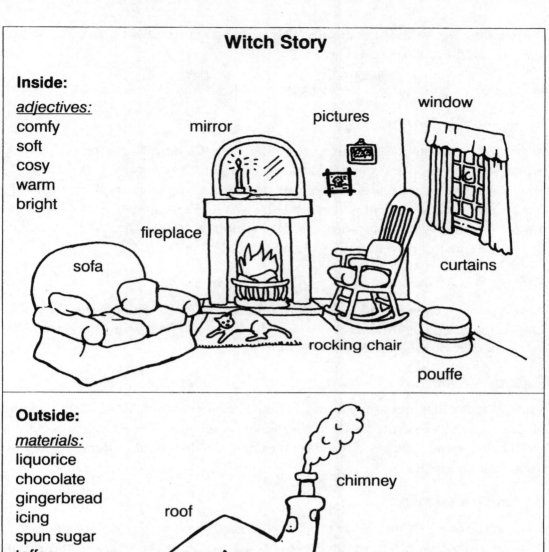

mirror

pictures

window

fireplace

sofa

curtains

rocking chair

pouffe

Outside:

materials:
liquorice
chocolate
gingerbread
icing
spun sugar
toffee
nougat
candy

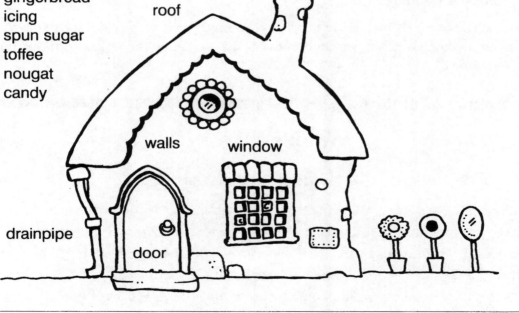

chimney

roof

walls

window

drainpipe

door

the oven, Gretel shoved her inside. The wicked creature was burned to a crisp and the children made their escape.

In the story, the writer has to invert the story and make the witch the hero.

Paragraph 1 (opening)

Begin with the witch. We want to turn her into the hero of the piece, so let's exaggerate the goodness of her character. Give her a sweet name (Daisy, Molly). Show her at home with lots of domestic details (rocking chair, roaring log fire). How do we describe a dear, sweet old lady? What pet would she have? (Keep in mind she was a witch in the original.) What hobbies might she have? How did her home come to be made of confectionery?

Paragraph 2 (complication)

Now describe Hansel and Gretel. You might want to change their names. Emphasise their naughtiness. What can they be doing? How are they dressed? What do they do when they see the house?

Paragraph 3 (action)

The old lady challenges the children about their behaviour. Write an exchange of dialogue between them. How should it be set out? The teacher needs to model this section clearly. How do you show defiance and rudeness short of using bad language?

Paragraph 4 (resolution)

What is the best resolution for this story? Does the old lady really have magical powers? Do the children get their come-uppance? How do we get humour out of the ending?

Examples of children's work

Winnie's Story

By Damiak Jukka, Year 3

It all began when a big red slimy, sticky tongue poked through my wall. Twisting round and round making the hole bigger and bigger, the tongue was like a snake. I was amazed, furious. I sprinted round the corner. There was a boy and a girl. They said, "Clear off witch!" I felt frustrated.

Black, grey smoke started coming out of my ears. Lightning flashed in my eyes. I was fuming. My clothes turned black then I began shaking. At that moment I felt a pointed hat on my head. It was a witch's hat! Then a broom floated towards me. It went to my hand and I grabbed tight hold of the broom. I was like the queen of witches. I felt I was going crazy in my mind.

Then the children stood in amazement. Then I tapped the boy and girl on the head. They ran away. They never ate sweets again.

The little old lady

By Lyndsey Lee, Year 6

Once upon a time in a lonely wood, was a little old lady called Winnie. She had a pet budgie called Charlie. Charlie was a very special budgie because he sang with Winnie when she was upset. What Winnie used to do is get up early, go downstairs and knit some sweaters for poor children. She also used to do bingo for the elderly people in the rest home. The favourite thing she liked was flowers. She had flowers everywhere. She used to spend most of her time on her own, that's how she liked it.

She really respected her house. It was one of the most weirdest houses I've seen anywhere. The walls were made out of Cadburys chocolate, the roof was made out of very thick candy-floss. The door was made out of a giant jelly baby and the chimney was made out of a flump. Winnie was just sitting on her chair and she heard a noise. So she turned around to see what it was. She looked out of the window and there was two cheeky kids Hansel and Gretel.

Winnie went to the door and shouted, "Hey who are you, go away and stop eating my house! It took a long time to build that."

"Why should we go away? It's scrumptious," said Hansel.

"I'll call the police if you don't go away within fifty seconds!" yelled Winnie.

"Yeh yeh" the kids both said as they walked away laughing.

Winnie went back into her half eaten house and phoned her friend and told her what had happened and said that she was glad of what she said to them!

Comments

The first piece of work is from Year 3. This is a simplified version for younger children. Here, we begin with Hansel's tongue poking through the wall. The child writes in the first person, describing the scene. The tone is engaging and reflects the enthusiasm she puts into her writing. All too often we ask young children to re-tell traditional tales. This is a real secretarial chore because there is so much patterned language and repetition in many of these stories. Is it really worth putting them off by making them toil through, say, the Billy Goats Gruff, and all that tripping and trapping? Why not just describe the Troll at the bridge? Better to take an excerpt and concentrate on quality language than to labour through the whole story and disenchant the youngster. (See pp. 111–12 for examples.)

In the Year 3 sample there is a confident story opening: 'It all began with a big, red, slimy, sticky tongue …' Description is strong: 'the tongue was like a snake.' The objective for a follow-up lesson might be to introduce more complex sentence structures:

- The tongue, twisting and curling, licked its way through the wall.
- Heart thudding, I sprinted round the corner.

The children's work itself gives the teacher a pathway to future planning.

Lyndsey, in Year 6, writes a lively, endearing piece. It uses paragraphing effectively and dialogue is set out correctly. The beginning and ending is suitable to the subject matter.

In re-drafting, a couple of points could be taken up, the formulation 'most weirdest' for example. Areas could be starred for further investigation. After 'She had flowers everywhere' Lyndsey could spend a few sentences exploring the colours and perfume of the flowers to strengthen the sensory impact of the story. Similarly she could exploit the house of sweets, though the detail of the chimney as a flump is wonderful.

A follow-up lesson might be to re-tell Jack and the Beanstalk, in which the giant is a kindly individual and Jack is a mischievous thief. Again, dialogue should be a central focus. The teacher needs to demonstrate both the mechanics of dialogue (punctuation) and its dynamics (listen to the ways people talk to one another).

Paragraph 1 (opening): The kindly giant is saving up for his holiday. Where would he go? Wicked Jack steals his money. Describe the giant's feelings of sadness and frustration. Describe the sound of Jack's voice. What verbs will you select to demonstrate mischief?

Paragraph 2 (problem): The giant tries to stop Jack taking his hen. Maybe he is afraid of heights and can't follow him down the beanstalk.

Paragraph 3 (action): He chases after Jack to save his harp, slips and falls after Jack. Again, what verbs do you select to show him plummeting earthwards?

Paragraph 4 (resolution): How would this end? Narrative is often a chain of problem-solving decisions. So get solving.

Lesson 3

An adventure story

Working title: *Stranded in the jungle*

Lesson Plan

Objective: to write a piece of narrative fiction, using techniques of tension.

Stimulus: discussion of a helicopter crash in the jungle. Possibly show an excerpt of the film *Black Hawk Down* to show how a helicopter comes down.

Sentence level: complex sentences.

Shared writing: a helicopter goes out of control. Writing the scene in a way that involves the reader.

Guided writing: continue the story, as a tale of survival.

Structure of the lesson

Paragraph 1 (opening)

Begin with the helicopter flying over the jungle canopy. There should be visual description of the sky and the rainforest. Describe the sky, mist, trees, river. What adjectives will you select? Next, what sounds, smells, sights would you be aware of as the helicopter goes out of control, as it bumps through the treetops and finally hits the ground? Don't forget the sound of the rotor blades, the sound of the branches against the fuselage. This vocabulary may need teaching. What goes through your mind as the ground rushes up?

Paragraph 2 (problem)

Do you lose consciousness? Where has the craft landed, in a river, in the rooftops, in quicksand? What is the scene inside the cabin? Do you smell petrol? Is it bitter, acrid, pungent? Is anyone hurt? Describe them. How do you get out? Choose verbs carefully. Is it easy? Describe sweat, straining limbs, aching muscles.

Stranded in the Jungle

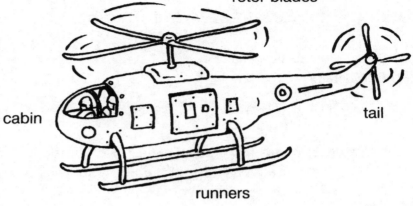

rotor blades

helicopter
chopper

cabin

tail

runners

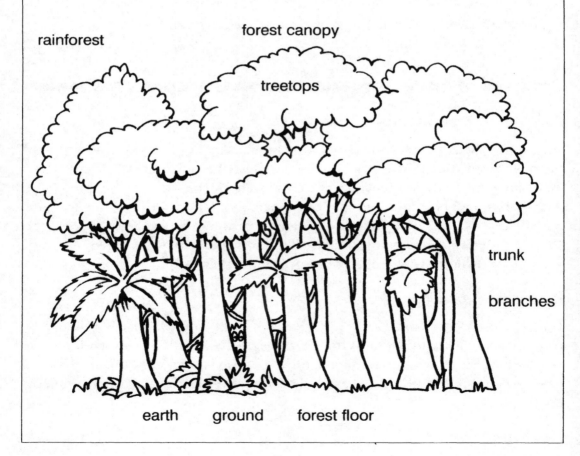

rainforest

forest canopy

treetops

trunk

branches

earth   ground   forest floor

Comments

Dominic and Daniel use visual imagery well and pace the story effectively. They incorporate subordinate clauses to make their sentences resonant: e.g. 'Below us, stretching as far as the eye can see, an emerald green plain of tree tops.' In class discussion the teacher could point out where to put the commas and highlight the subordinate clause in different coloured pens. She could ask if adding a verb strengthens the effect: 'Below us, stretching as far as the eye can see, *there is* an emerald green plain of tree tops.'

What follows should be a discussion of where to add descriptive touches to strengthen the reader's visualisation of the scene. Open questioning is most effective:

- What did the rotor blades look like? Were they mangled, twisted?
- What creatures did you see?
- Were the passengers wounded?
- What did they say to each other?

This need not mean the child re-drafting. The teacher could have the text on an interactive whiteboard and re-draft for the children, displaying how to layer the text, adding description, dialogue and detail to develop a stronger impact on the audience.

A follow-up might be an avalanche story in which a climber is buried in an avalanche and has to dig himself out and crawl to safety with damaged legs. (There are true stories of this kind of survival tale. It is easy to see how this could be structured.)

Paragraph 1: the avalanche from first rumblings to landslide.

Paragraph 2: buried alive.

Paragraph 3: digging your way out.

Paragraph 4: the crawl to safety.

There are obvious cross curricular extensions to this type of story:

- Tell the story of a follower of Boudicca in the final battle against the Romans.
- Tell a story of a sailor on the *Mary Rose*.
- Tell the story of a child trapped in a house during the Blitz. He is pinned by an unexploded bomb.
- Tell the story of a Victorian chimney sweep caught in a fall of soot (see *The Climbing Boys* by Alan Gibbons, Collins Pathways).
- Tell the story of a refugee arriving in a new country (see *The Other Side of Truth* by Beverley Naidoo).

Lesson 4

A bullying story

Working title: *Bully*

Lesson Plan

Objective: to write a bullying story, selecting words and phrases that describe scenes. Present dialogue in stories.

Stimulus: excerpts from *Chicken* by Alan Gibbons.

Sentence level: strong verbs, dialogue.

Shared writing: an exchange of dialogue.

Guided writing: develop a story about a new child in school.

Extract from *Chicken* by Alan Gibbons

The term's first rounders match had got me off to a bad start, of course. I remember Webbo yelling "Get it!" Well, how was I to know Lianne Whalley would sky the ball straight at me just when I was busy watching the seagulls pecking the leftover crisps off the Infants' yard? I didn't ask to be in the vital place at the last match-deciding moment. Five rounders each and only my hands between victory and defeat.

"Catch the thing!" bawled Webbo as he raced towards me. I didn't, of course. I tried. I stuck out my hands and did my best to cup them under the ball. I suppose my big chance to be a hero was just too much for me. I closed my eyes and hoped for the best, but the ball popped out of my hands as easily as it had dropped in. Lianne completed the rounder with her arms raised in triumph, while Pete Moran laughed himself sick at my attempt at a catch. Webbo wasn't laughing. He only played to win, and I'd just scuppered his hopes. Webbo didn't like being on the losing side – *ever.*

"You," hissed Webbo, prodding a finger into my chest. "You are dead."

No, he definitely did not like being on the losing side. I looked around. Nobody was listening, nobody except Craig, and he just grimaced sympathetically.

"Try to keep out of Webbo's way," he advised on the way back into school.

That was easier said than done. I'd realised on my first day since the move from Yorkshire a few months back that Webbo and I weren't going to get on.

"Hey, Woollyback," he had shouted in the playground.

I must have looked blank.

"Yes, you," he said. "Don't you know what a Woollyback is?"

I shook my head. That was a mistake.

"Well, soft lad," explained Webbo. "It's like this. There are two kinds of people in the world, Scousers and Woollybacks. If you don't come from Liverpool then you're a Woollyback. You're not from Liverpool are you?"

No, I wasn't. I'd finally discovered that I had something in common with Michael Jackson, Arnold Schwarzenegger, the Pope and Mother Theresa of Calcutta – we're all Woollybacks.

"So now you understand, don't you. Woollyback?"

I nodded and turned to walk away. Carl O'Rourke barred my way.

"Who said you could go?" demanded Webbo.

"Nobody," I admitted. Silly me, I didn't know I needed permission!

"Then you wait until you're told you can go," said Webbo. "Understand?"

"Yes," I murmured nervously. "I understand."

"Hear that?" announced Webbo to Carl and his other mate, Vinny Boyle. "This Woollyback understands Scouse. It looks like we won't need that interpreter after all."

Vinny and Carl sneered. I managed a thin smile.

"Off you go then, Woolly," ordered Webbo.

I turned to go, but Webbo took my leg from under me with a trip: I sprawled full-length on the playground, skinning my elbow, setting off hoots of laughter behind me.

"Clumsy aren't they, these Woollybacks?" snorted Vinny.

"It's living up hills that does it," said Webbo. "It makes their feet a funny shape."

I turned my funny-shaped feet towards the classroom and vowed to stay out of Webbo's way.

Unfortunately, in a school the size of Bride Lane that was easier said than done. I've seen sardine tins that are less cramped.

"A penny for them," said Mum as we reached the front gate.

Her voice wrenched me out of my gloomy thoughts. "What?"

"You mean 'pardon'," corrected Mum. Once in a while she would get on her high horse about talking properly. By the time she'd reminded me to say 'pardon' instead of 'what', I'd forgotten what she wanted in the first place.

"What?" I repeated lamely.

"Stop saying 'what' all the time," said Mum. She was getting exasperated. "I was checking whether you were still with us. You've been really quiet. Are you sure you're all right?"

"Of course I'm sure," I snapped. "Just because our Anna never shuts up, doesn't mean I have to be the same."

Structure of the lesson

Paragraph 1 (opening)

It is your first day at school. How do you feel? You meet the bullies. What do they say? What do they do? Is the bullying verbal or physical? It should be low-key at first and build through the story. Writers have a gear box, so don't start in top gear. You will exhaust your reader! Take care to set out dialogue correctly. The teacher can use his professional judgement to decide just how much dialogue each group is capable of.

Paragraph 2 (problem)

The bullying carries on during the day. Do they warn you not to grass? How do they stop you telling an adult? How do you feel? Are you distracted from your work? Does the teacher ask what's wrong? How do you answer?

Paragraph 3 (action)

To build tension, describe the victim's feelings overnight. How can we show the worry and anxiety they feel? Internal monologue, etc. What physical reactions do they suffer as they look forward to the next day and facing the bullies again? Why don't they tell their parents?

Paragraph 4 (resolution)

How is the bullying resolved? Take care to keep it realistic. What are the options?
• Stand up for yourself. How?
• Make friends and develop security in a group.
• Tell an adult. What do they do?

Finally, describe your feelings and the reaction of the bullies after it is resolved.

Bully

By Rebecca Jones, Year 3

The moment I arrived at my new school, the bullying started. The bully was in year 6, two years older than me. As he walked up to me he said, "I'm Tom, you're dead." "Oh," I replied. That was all I could say. I started shaking like a leaf, my stomach was churning. I felt sick. He started pushing me and pinching me. He did anything he could to hurt me. All through the lesson I could only think about play-time and Tom. My blood ran cold, my heart was pounding. I felt worse than sick. I felt like running away but I wasn't going to do that. Well that's what I felt like but I didn't know what I was in for ...

At play-time it all started again, but worse. Tom and his gang walked over to me, "You're dead remember." "Cool" I said, trying to be cool. They just laughed. "Trying to be cool are you?" they asked. It was as if they could see inside my head. They kicked me and called me names like nerd and geek. They also gave me a black eye and an awful lot of bruises. In class I couldn't concentrate. I just kept glancing at the clock for home time and Miss Waters, our teacher, but when she glanced at me I just pretended to be thinking. All that was in my book was a date and a title.

At home that night Mum asked me "How did you get the black eye, eh?" "Oh," I began, "I walked into, erm, the, er, book case." "Really" she replied. "Mum" I said, "do you ..." "Don't worry, I'm here if you need me," she interrupted. I walked up the stairs to my room. Parents never understand do they?

The next morning I decided, this has got to stop. I know what I'll do to stop it as well. Right through the day they picked on me and for the next two weeks it carried on. I thought my plan wasn't working. Then a miracle occurred — they asked me to join their gang. My plan had worked. It was to ignore them. Now we're best mates!

Comments

Rebecca's story is very mature for a Year 3 child. She is using paragraphing and dialogue effectively. A teaching point might be to stress that new dialogue should begin on a new line, but this is a minor quibble.

Once more, using this story as a template, the teacher could, using an interactive whiteboard, show where the writer could strengthen the story. The section about how the main character worries overnight about the bullying to come the next day would benefit from a little re-drafting. Again, questioning is the main strategy:

- How did the character feel? Did her stomach churn? Did she toss and turn in bed?
- What about her thoughts? Did she talk to herself in the bathroom mirror? Could we use internal monologue?

Such questioning can deepen the child's understanding of plot development.

The applications of this kind of story in Personal and Social Education lessons are obvious.

Other subjects for this kind of story, depending on the age of the children, could be:

- loneliness
- ganging up (see *Ganging Up* by Alan Gibbons, Dolphin Paperbacks)
- breaking friends and making up again
- girlfriend/boyfriend trouble (See *Julie and Me and Michael Owen Makes Three* by Alan Gibbons, Dolphin paperbacks)
- peer pressure
- disagreements with parents
- racism (See *Caught in the Crossfire, Whose Side Are You On?* and *The Edge*, all by Alan Gibbons, Dolphin paperbacks)

Lesson 5

A memory

Working title: *First day at school*

Lesson Plan

    Objective: to write a fictional personal recollection.

    Stimulus: discussion of memories; excerpts of memoirs from fiction or non-fiction.

    Sentence level: variety of punctuation to reflect the content (capital letters, commas, exclamation marks, question marks, parentheses).

    Shared writing: getting started – grabbing the reader's attention.

    Guided writing: continuing the recollection, involving your reader in the story.

Structure of the lesson

This is a shorter piece, so I have made it a two paragraph structure.

Paragraph 1

Remind the class of the idea of tension, locking away the key element in the story in a metaphorical steel safe in your cerebral cortex.

Demonstrate how they could develop their story without giving away the main idea, that it is the first day at school. Describe how people are acting, how you are feeling, what people have told you about this thing. Get the reader to guess from your clues. Use questions to ask whether it will be a positive or negative experience. At the end of the paragraph you can let the cat out of the bag, but not the child out of school!

One narrative tool employed in the sample of children's work below is 'triples'. This is using three adjectives together for effect (e.g. 'I was warm, happy, comfortable.'

Paragraph 2

Again, ask questions. When did your character meet their first teacher? What were they like in looks or personality? How did she greet you? (Teaching point: do you need to model speech marks for the class?)

What did your mum do? How did you feel? What was the school like inside? What did you say at the end of the day? Did you want to come back?

Finally, don't forget, the two most important lines in your story could be the first and the last. Leave the children with a sense of satisfaction, of a conclusion that will stay with them.

Examples of children's work

A memory ...

By Vikki Jones, Year 5

There I was trembling, uncertainly biting my lip. I walked down Maryville Road to the big iron gates. All the kids told me it's a living nightmare. You're trapped there listening to someone going on and on about one boring thing (I think the thing is sums and sentences). Would this thing or person be nice, kind and helpful or ignorant, mean and evil? It was my first day at school. Yes, school!!

I stood glancing quickly sideways behind me and in front. Then I saw a lady smiling happily. She was saying, "Can class RG line up please," she said. Then my Mum dragged me towards the lady's line and pushed me into it. My face grew into a sad face. Was my Mum getting rid of me? No, she wouldn't. Well only for six hours nearly every day for about seven years!

Comments

Victoria's work is full of playful humour. It also uses the full range of punctuation to get its point across. A piece of work like this can be used to demonstrate punctuation *in context*, as a genuine guide to meaning.

In class discussion the next lesson the teacher could highlight areas to be corrected (in paragraph 2 Vikki uses 'she said' twice in a sentence when once is fine). More importantly, she could use some of Victoria's narrative techniques as examples:

- the use of triples: three adjectives used for emphasis. In this case Vikki counter-poses two triples: 'Would this thing or person be nice, kind and helpful or ignorant, mean and evil?'
- the use of tension, holding back what the first day is until the end
- the use of a telling last line to sum up the whole piece of work
- the use of parentheses to make an aside: ('I think the thing is sums and sentences')

Vikki's story is a model of such writing.

Other memoirs could include:
- a favourite holiday
- my pet
- the happiest day of my life
- my worst nightmare

or simply give free choice.

Teachers will need to be sensitive. I taught a Year 5 child once (in a different school from Vikki's) who interrupted me during the introduction to this lesson to say, 'Mr Gibbons, I don't remember ever having a happy day in my life.'

I have to confess, it was one of the few times in my teaching career when I was genuinely lost for words.

Lesson 6

Novelising a play

Working title: *The witches*

Lesson Plan

    Objective: to produce a modern re-telling of a known play, *Macbeth* by William Shakespeare.

    Stimulus: the witches' scene from *Macbeth* (Act I, Scene 3).

  Sentence level: to adapt texts for particular readers and purposes.

  Shared writing: the setting.

  Guided writing: introduce the main characters.

Structure of the lesson

As in Lesson 5, this usually breaks down best into two paragraphs: the one in which the witches gather round the cauldron, and the one in which Macbeth and Banquo appear. The teacher should, of course, exercise her professional judgement. The activity can easily be extended.

Paragraph 1

Describe the heath, the gorse, the rocks, the bare trees. Describe the witches, their clothes, their faces, the cauldron. Use metaphor/simile to make it vivid.

You might also want to use personification to compare the witches with their environment (e.g. 'the bare branches were like claws': 'the scrub grass was like the thin hair on an ancient scalp'.)

Paragraph 2

Introduce the warriors. They are fresh from battle. How do they look? Focus on weapons, armour. Describe the blood on their clothing, armour. How do they react to the witches? What do the witches say in reply? Remind the class about setting out dialogue correctly. Demonstrate. A useful strategy is to write the narrative section (*The witch said*) in one colour, the words she actually said (*All Hail, Macbeth*) in another colour and the punctuation in a third one. This kind of visual cue helps the children internalise punctuation conventions.

Macbeth

inky stormclouds   dark skies   rain

armour
swords
shields

Macbeth
Banquo on horseback
mounted riders

smoke
cauldron
fire

three witches
crones
figures
women

rocks
boulders

heather

gorse   furze

The Witches

By Heather Davies, Year 6

The witches gathered in the driving storm. Thunder boomed and lightening lit up the sky like a light bulb. The ragged heath was deserted and scattered with jagged boulders. The trees were as dead as the spirits of soldiers. The witches cackled as they cast a spell. They had claws and long beards. They were shrivelled like prunes and their bones stuck out.

Two warriors rode into view. They were Macbeth and Banquo. The pair were blood stained and their weapons blunt. They were fresh from battle. The two spotted the witches and drew their weapons. They were horrified. The witches started to chant. "We promise you will be Thane of Cawdor," chanted the first. "And King of Scotland," finished the second.

Comments

Heather's description in this short scene is excellent. To develop in re-drafting the teacher could ask:
- How did the rain fall? Did it dimple tiny puddles? Did it skip off the scree?
- Could we make more of the witches' appearance?
- What were their eyes like?
- How did their clothes hang?
- Furthermore, what about the reactions of Macbeth and Banquo?
- Did they shrink back in disgust?
- Did Macbeth feel a frisson of ambition?

A further teaching point to build on what she has done might be to demonstrate how one or two subordinate clauses could add texture and relief to an engaging piece of work. For example: 'Mired in gore and wild-eyed with the horrors they had witnessed, they came fresh from battle.'

A related activity might be to do the reverse operation and turn an excerpt from a novel into a play. This kind of work helps develop mental agility and gives the children confidence to work in different genres.

Other possible novelisations might be:
- the appearance of Banquo at the feast
- the death of Julius Caesar (cross curricular links are obvious)
- the appearance of the ghost in *Hamlet*
- Hamlet's indecision over killing the King.

Lesson 7

Writing an adventure

Working title: *Batman foils bank raid!*

Lesson Plan

Objective: to write a first person narrative.

Stimulus: short excerpt from a Batman movie.

Sentence level: correct use of verb tenses – present tense.

Shared writing: a first person report, similar to a news reporter.

Guided writing: continue, maintaining the present tense.

Structure of the lesson

The example on page 67 is from a Year 4 pupil. Repeated higher in the school, the activity could be longer and more sustained.

Paragraph 1 (opening)

You are standing outside the bank. What do you see and hear as the robbery takes place? Use similes to describe the shots, the muffled screams.

Paragraph 2 (problem)

Give the children a sketch of the getaway driver and the robber. Ask them to write a detailed description.

Paragraph 3 (action)

How does Batman appear? Can you use an effective simile to show the caped crusader? How do you show the action? It is best to imagine it in slow motion and break down the process e.g. 'A fist whistled past Batman's ear. The caped crusader rocked back on his heels, pivoted on one foot and slammed a punch into his opponent's stomach.' This is better than: 'He socked him one.'

Paragraph 4 (resolution)

Describe the arrest and the arrival of the police. What do you see and hear (sirens etc)? Don't forget a telling last line.

The Bank Robbery

bank

alarm screeching

windows

door

case
box of cash

bank robber

passers by
pedestrians

getaway car
driver

Batman foils bank raid!

By Hollie Turner, Year 4

I am standing in Eccleston Street, Prescot, outside the NatWest bank. Overhead I can see six gangsters in pairs. In each pair one of them is armed. I can see two on the roof of the bank in case the robbery goes wrong. The two armed gangsters on the roof can rob the bank and kill whoever's in charge of it. The gangsters are getting ready to shoot.

Hang on! What's this? There's something floating on the rooftop and it looks like a black binbag. No it's not, it looks like a super hero. He's got the two off the roof top. Now he's got the other six and reported them to the police. We are safe again now because he or it has saved us.

Your reporter Hollie Turner.

Comments ■■■■■■■■■■■■■■■■■■■■■■■■■■■■■■■■■■■

Hollie's image of the black bin bag is very striking. The more she can employ this kind of visual imagery the better. In order to extend this short story, either with this Year 4 class or later in the school, certain strategies could be used:

- In order to pace the story, give the children a sketch of the robbers. Ask the children to give short descriptions of them. Remember Stephen King's adage that 'Description starts in the mind of the writer and ends in the reader's.'
- When Hollie says the gangsters are getting ready to shoot, *how* do they get ready? Do they drop into a crouch? Do they draw their weapons? Do they shout something?
- Could the confrontation between Batman and the gangsters be extended? Maybe bullets could ping off his body armour. The swirl of his black cloak could be described, like a raven's wings perhaps. The teacher's role is to demonstrate how the effect of the story can be strengthened by weaving in more detail, more incident. It is all about breaking action down into a series of freeze frames. Each frame becomes a sentence.

Extensions of this short piece of writing are obvious. You could use a computer programme to make a mock-up front page of the local newspaper.

There are plenty of other ideas in the same vein:
- Mummy escapes from the local museum
- Bird attack on the local town

Cross-curricular opportunities include:
- a first hand account of the Battle of Salamis, Thermopylae, Marathon, Hastings. ('This is Mary Jones reporting from Senlac Hill, Hastings. Now back to the studio.')
- a flood
- a famine

Eye of the world

Mummy stalks Prescot!

By your reporter Lauren Joinson, Year 4

A Mummy is at large in Prescot.

Sometime in the early hours of Tuesday morning an Egyptian mummy escaped from its sarcophagus. I have watched video coverage of the event.

The mummy emerged out of the sarcophagus. The security guard started to walk backwards towards the door. But suddenly the mummy lifted him up off the ground and snapped his head off. The mummy smashed through the windows.

Eye-witness Holly Dingsdale was on her way home from the nightshift at McDonald's. She told me what happened:

"This policeman was watching out until the mummy came up to him and started to strangle him, and then squeezed his neck. Blood was spurting out like a river. Then I saw it break a car into shreds with his bare hands."

But daylight didn't bring an end to the mayhem. He turned up at Prescot County Primary School. He strangled Mr Jorgensen to the guts. We were all on the playground when we saw it. We had to run to safety. But Sam Murphy got caught. As I write the creature remains at large.

Bird attack on Prescot!

By our on the spot reporter, Thomas Furlong, Year 4

Yesterday Prescot looked on in horror at the extraordinary events. Here is a diary of the remarkable scenes I witnessed. At 10.45am in Prescot County Primary School playground two hawks and a raven swooped down and attacked three children. Teachers led children into classrooms. The three birds then attacked the windows.

At 11.30am in Eccleston Street it was now the turn of the midday shoppers. Fifteen hawks dived down and injured people. Humans hid under buses and cars. Dogs were barking madly and places were being brought down and were crashing. People used umbrellas to stop the birds attacking.

12 noon. Reports were coming in of further attacks all over Merseyside. The Liver buildings were being held up by the attacks. The fire brigade fired water what was not helpful.

Early evening: as we went to press the attacks had ended and it is a day that will go down in history.

Lesson 8

Narrative description

Working title: *The Storm*

Lesson Plan

    Objective: to write the story of a natural event, a storm, understanding the difference between prose and poetry.

    Stimulus: short excerpt of a film showing a storm at sea e.g. *A Perfect Storm* or *The Guns of Navarone*.

Sentence level: subordinate clauses, personification.

Shared writing: demonstrate how to describe the storm rising.

Guided writing: continue the story of the storm.

Structure of the lesson

The structure follows the pattern of the storm. It rises, it peaks, it subsides. Conventionally, using personification, you might describe the rise as toddler-like, the peak as adult-like, and the subsiding as reminiscent of old age. In the example below the writer Beverley plays with the convention and creates something original.

Paragraph 1 (opening)

Use personification. Describe the breeze, the rain, the stormy skies. What similes and metaphors can you use? You could describe the raindrops dimpling the waves or the clouds scudding across an inky sky. Make it visual and auditory. What do you see and hear? The point is to use words to paint a picture in the readers mind.

Paragraph 2 (climax)

Describe the storm breaking over the city. What does it do? What's it like when it encounters buildings, people? How will personification work here? Is the storm mischievous, raging, out of control? What verbs or adjectives will you use to express this? Can you use place names to add to the effect, making it local to your school? Teaching point: what connectives do you use? Phrases work better than single words (e.g. Reaching its crescendo, the storm crashes over the city).

Storm

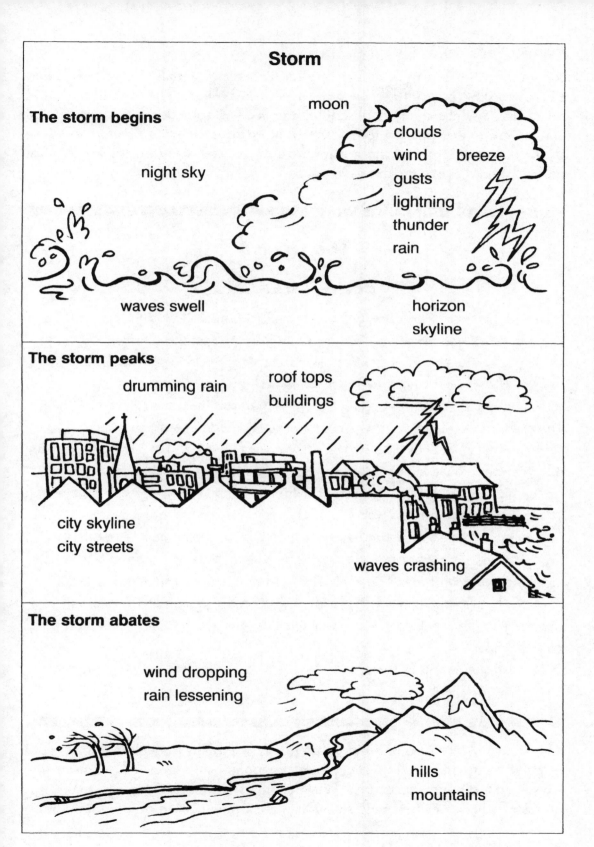

The storm begins

moon

night sky

clouds

wind   breeze

gusts

lightning

thunder

rain

waves swell

horizon

skyline

The storm peaks

drumming rain

roof tops

buildings

city skyline

city streets

waves crashing

The storm abates

wind dropping

rain lessening

hills

mountains

Paragraph 3 (resolution)

Remember connectives or connecting sentences (e.g. 'Finally, all passion spent, the storm slips away'). Describe how the storm subsides. The tone here should be elegiac. You are, after all, describing the death of something. A short clip you could show to describe the tone is the Hallowe'en scene from *Fantasia*, followed by the dawn. Where does the storm slink away to? Can you think of a telling last line? It should evoke death or old age.

Examples of children's work

The Storm

By Beverley Wade, Year 8

It is midnight, the dead of night, out at sea. The wind is rising and sounds like a distant god breathing heavily. I can hear the raindrops dropping into the icy sea. The waves are shining like a throbbing vein inside you. It's like a herd of crazed white horses stampeding with anger

The impactive storm is raging like a rolling barrel heading for the Pierhead. The old tramps sleeping on the cold Merseyside streets are scattering to find an empty doorplace to be their home for the night. The storm is getting mischievious, rattling the doors of nearby buildings like a thief in the middle of the night. Milk bottles are rolling from the steps of houses and clattering. There is no peace for the workers of the city.

Finally, as the storm abates, the rain is just dropping gently to the ground. The storm is just like a toddler having a terrible tantrum but is now tired and weak and ready to rest. The wind has dropped and is now like a newborn baby breathing lightly whilst it is sleeping peacefully. The sun is starting to show behind the tall buildings, a shy kitten finally showing itself to the public.

At last the storm is over.

Comments

This is a very evocative piece of writing. It is essentially a prose poem. It could be used to discuss the difference between poetry and prose, to explore line length and sentence structure. What changes would we need to make this unmistakeably a poem? Could the class write a poem based on the same idea?

Using Beverley's work as an example, the teacher could highlight the various important features:

- Using subordinate clauses not as a dull grammatical construct but in order to create an evocative mood.
- Using personification to sustain a central image throughout the piece.
- Using a familiar place as a backdrop. In re-drafting, the city's sights and sounds could be explored in even greater detail. Cities often have their own mythology. Think of Inspector Rebus' Edinburgh or Dickens' London. The use of proper nouns, of particularly striking places, can add depth to a descriptive story.

Other descriptive pieces along the same lines might be:

- The four seasons (*stimulus: Vivaldi*)
- Morning (*stimulus: Grieg*)
- First sight of New York through the mist (*stimulus: Dvorak: The New World Symphony*)
- The planets (*stimulus: Holst: The Planets*)

Teaching point: music is a particularly appropriate stimulus for descriptive writing. What's more, an assembly in which the writer reads their work against the background of the music that inspired it can be both memorable and emotive.

Lesson 9

A cliff-hanger story

Working title: *High Rise!*

Lesson Plan

Objective: to write an adventure story, using the principles of tension.

Stimulus: discussion of fear of heights, photos of tower blocks. Alternatively, a short drama session. Draw a chalk line to represent the ledge. How does it feel to stand on tiptoe for two minutes, five, longer?

Sentence level: internal monologue.

Shared writing: a gripping opening.

Guided writing: continue the story, maintaining tension.

Structure of the lesson

Paragraph 1 (opening)

Imagine you are in a room. Out in the corridor there is a fire. What do you smell, hear, taste, see? How do you wake up? Think of the verbs used to represent eyes opening quickly (e.g. *snapped, flicked*). Short sentences work well to create drama and tension. What forces you to retreat to the window and consider climbing outside, thirty metres above the ground? If you want to represent motivation in a story, you have to show it. Did a jet of flame race towards you? Did flame belch suddenly into the room? Were you going woozy because of the smoke?

Paragraph 2 (problem)

How do you climb out of the window? Draw a diagram for the children to demonstrate the problem. Fiction is often a matter of analysing a problem then solving it. How do you get out of the window? How does the brickwork or masonry feel? Does it hurt your bare feet? What are you thinking? How do you show fear of heights? Describe the earth below? (e.g. *The earth swam. The ground rushed up towards me*). How do you show the reader just how precarious your situation is? Physical feelings (e.g. *My fingers gouged into the masonry*)? Descriptions of fear (e.g. *Sweat ran down my spine*)?

High Rise!

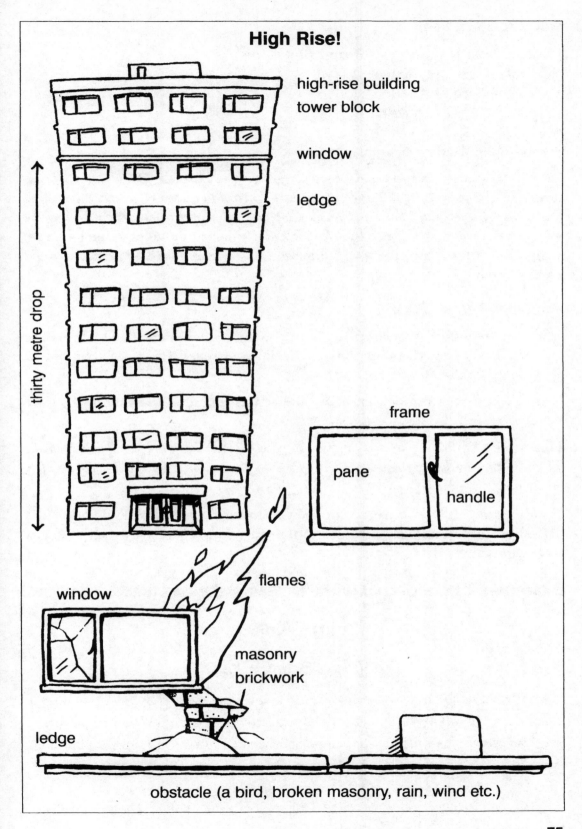

high-rise building
tower block

window

ledge

thirty metre drop

frame

pane

handle

flames

window

masonry
brickwork

ledge

obstacle (a bird, broken masonry, rain, wind etc.)

Place an obstacle in the way of your protagonist:
- a broken section of ledge
- a nesting bird
- rain
- wind
- a swinging window cleaner's cradle.

Describe as tensely as you can how you get by the obstacle. Break the process down. (e.g. *The bird's beak pecked at my ankle. I tried to flick it away with my foot. It was no use. Kick at it too hard and I would topple from my precarious perch. Feeling the cold trickle of blood on my skin, I prayed for help.*) Internal monologue helps create sympathy for the main character's dilemma. (e.g. *Could I do this, I wondered, could I really do this?*)

Paragraph 4 (resolution)

Is it a closed ending (you climb to safety, you are hauled to safety on a fireman's ladder)? Don't forget to describe your feelings of relief (e.g. *Lying exhausted on the floor, joy flooded through me.*)

Would you prefer an open ending (the fire has spread to the window you are heading for)?

Finally, you could try a twist in the tale: *Unable to hang on, I toppled into the darkness. But, at the very moment I had given up hope, strong arms pulled me to safety on the long reach ladder.*

Teaching point: If you have rescue by the fireman, you should mention the arrival of the fire appliance earlier in the story to prepare the reader for just this eventuality.

Examples of children's work ▰▰▰▰▰▰▰▰▰▰▰▰

High Rise!

By Nicola Soutar, Year 7

It was the smoke that woke me. I jerked awake. My eyes snapped open wide. I could hear the whooping sound of the fire alarm. A halo grew up around my bed, the black-blue smoke crept under the door. The sour smoke was burning away at the back of my throat. Smoke was pouring through the cracks of the door. I tried to shout, but the smoke was filling up in my mouth. 'This is it,' I thought. 'How would I get out?' I climbed through the clouded smoke to get to the window. I was there, on the balcony. I reached back into the room for safety. That's when smoke billowed across the room. A jet of flame slid across the floor. There was no choice, there was no alternative.

My only option was to get to safety. I slowly placed my foot back onto the window ledge. A breeze of wind caught me, I felt the world was swinging. My other foot worked its way down the brickwork. I clung on with my toes. My fingers trembled with pain, clenching into the window frame. I felt like an eagle perched on the roof. I worked my way across step by step, inch by inch. As I dragged my feet along the bricks, the wind blowing into my eyes, I felt something pecking at my feet. I slowly turned my head to see what it was. A blackbird trying to feed its young. I tapped it, holding on with my life. Rain was tapping on my head. It got harder and harder. It started hail stoning. It got slippery, my hand slipped, I worked my way back up the bricks. The mortar crumbled. It fell to the ground below until it was like a dot on the floor.

I was on the edge of the balcony. I was there, I had to get on. My legs trembled, but I was there. I could still feel the heat. 'Why?' I thought. But there it was, licking through the door. It was the flames. It was back …

Comments

This example uses lots of vivid imagery and involves the reader in the character's predicament. The principle of 'Show, don't tell' is particularly relevant here.

In order to extend and deepen the dramatic impact of the fire the teacher could raise questions such as:
- Could you use the technique of personification for the fire or the smoke? Could you describe the fire as licking its way into the room or belching into the room? Could fingers of smoke scratch at the back of your throat or pepper your eyes with burning grains?
- Could you describe your muscles shrieking or buzzing with pain?
- How would you respond to the bird? You can't kick out or you will fall? Do you aim tentative flicks at it?
- How did you feel when the flames returned? Did horror claw at your insides?

This questioning process could help extend the story to a new level.

Other examples of this kind of story might be:
- Steeplejack (*stimulus: photos of workers on the Empire State Building*).
- The Deep: (*stimulus: excerpts from Jaws*).

Lesson 10

A possessed object story

Working title: *The Plymouth Fury*

Lesson Plan

Objective: to write a story using the principles of tension.

Stimulus: discussion of *Christine* by Stephen King (*note*: for younger children the teacher should explain some of the elements of the story. Some of it is too challenging for pre-adolescents). The car in the story is a classic American car of the 1950s called a Plymouth Fury, and gives the story its title. In the novel, a young American man buys a classic second-hand car and customises it. The trouble is, it turns out to be haunted, and begins a trail of mayhem.

Sentence level: figurative language.

Shared writing: a gripping opening.

Guided writing: developing a story with pace and tension.

Structure of the lesson

Paragraph 1 (opening)

To build tension we hide the demon car in the garage. What sounds do you hear (e.g. *the dull rumble of the engine, the rattle of the exhaust*)? What do you smell (e.g. *acrid fumes which make you gag*)? How do you feel (e.g. *At the sound of that whining, drumming engine I felt the hairs on the back of my neck prickle*)? Do you see the smoke, the glow of headlamps under the door?

Paragraph 2 (problem)

The garage doors open. Think of a dramatic first line (e.g. *That's when I saw it, the face of the vehicle*). Describe the car. A good aid to the children's imagination would be a labelled diagram of the front of the car. Use personification (e.g. the headlamps as eyes, the radiator grille as a mouth).

Plymouth Fury

Before we see the car

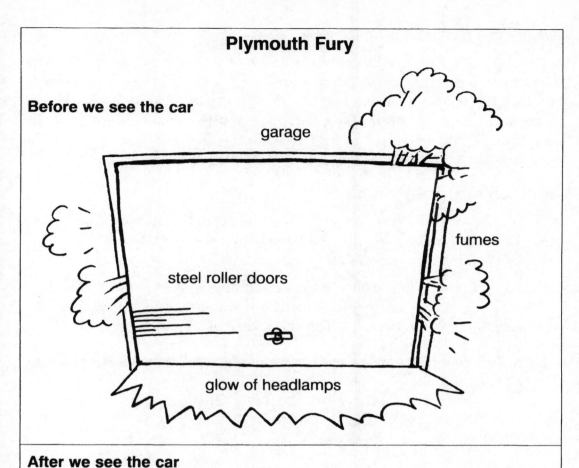

garage

fumes

steel roller doors

glow of headlamps

After we see the car

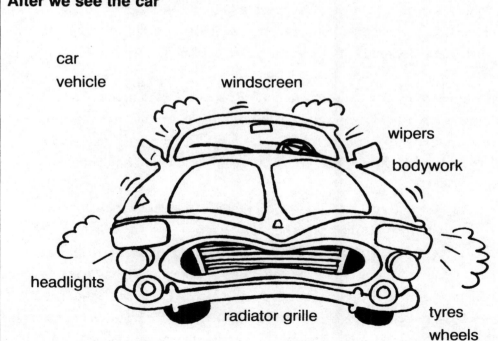

car

vehicle

windscreen

wipers

bodywork

headlights

radiator grille

tyres

wheels

Paragraph 3 (action)

Maybe the next day. Ask the pupils to think of a reason the main character might have to get into the car (Mum's handbag, a CD). It has to be plausible to convince the reader. Describe how the demon car traps them inside. Use as much detail as possible (e.g. *The seatbelt snapped across my chest, digging into the flesh, squeezing the breath out of me*). Describe an invisible hand moving the gear stick.

Paragraph 4 (resolution)

A wild drive as the car tries to destroy you. Go through the gears metaphorically, building tension, and literally, accelerating. Make it vivid (e.g. *I could feel the suspension rock, hear the tyres squeal*).

How does it finish? Will you choose a closed ending (e.g you jump clear and the car bursts into flame) or do you prefer an open ending (e.g. you think it is destroyed but a month later you hear the roar of an engine behind you)?

Examples of children's work

The Plymouth Fury

By Ryan Parry, Year 7

It was behind the garage doors. The furious engine roared as if to tell me something. I could see lights beaming on and off, like lightning flashing on a dark night. Then: the smell of burning. I could see the smoke ascending to my window.

Music came to my ears, but it wasn't friendly, it was demonic. The smoke formed an evil face. My blood went cold with fear and a chill ran down my spine. How could it have come on by itself – was there a burglar inside my car? No. A burglar would try not to wake me up. This was something else, something sinister.

I had just realised that I had left the bill payments in the garage, where my car was. This was when I threw open the garage doors – all the lights, all the chaos had stopped. I saw the money in the car although I don't remember it being there. I got in the car. Suddenly the doors snapped shut and the seatbelt skilfully swerved around my opposing hands and locked me in the seat. The headlights beamed again. The engine screamed. An invisible hand shifted the gearstick and the car zoomed through the garage doors, smashing it down.

I felt the tyres rumbling underneath me. If the seatbelt hadn't kept me in the seat I would have gone soaring through the window. The gear shifted in third and I felt the car speed up.

'I must escape,' I thought. I pushed the button to undo the seatbelt but it only tightened around me. I reached for the glove box and inside I found a saw. I seized it and started to saw the seatbelt. The car went over a speed hump and the saw went under the seat. I just couldn't reach it. I noticed there was a small, sharp stone beside me, so I tried to use it on the seatbelt, but, as I looked through the windscreen I saw that the car was heading for a wall! The gear shifted into fourth and the car accelerated in fury. I scratched at the seatbelt with the stone and it snapped. I scrambled for the window and smashed at it. The gear went into fifth and the car got close to the wall. Finally the window splintered and I dived through it.

I opened my eyes and found myself outside a scrapyard. Millions of cars sat in the gloomy atmosphere. I looked behind me and saw the Plymouth Fury advancing on me then I looked back. I saw all the cars' headlights turn on, one by one ...

Comments

Ryan's story displays a command of tension. This gives the story a satisfying structure and pace. Relevant questioning here might include:

- In Paragraph 1, how did you feel? Did anxiety course through your veins? Did unease prickle across your skin?
- In Paragraph 2, could you choose a piece of music suitable to the theme, 'Bad Moon Rising' or 'Monster Mash' for example?
- Could you show the reader how you felt trapped in the car? What effect did the seat belt have on your breathing? Did you try to struggle free? Did you hack at the seat belt with a pair of scissors?

The character's response to the strange events involves the reader. What about their thoughts? Could you describe them through internal monologue, e.g. *Could this really be happening, I asked myself?*

In this way an already excellent piece of work could be strengthened.

Other stories along these lines might include:

- a demon computer
- poltergeists – objects that move by themselves

Lesson 11

A description of an event

Working title: *The entry of Christ into Prescot*

Lesson Plan

Objective: to describe an event involving an anachronistic element.

Stimulus: 'The Entry of Christ into Prescot' (*note:* this is at the teacher's discretion. Some of the images are not suitable for a very young audience).

Sentence level: first person, present tense narrative.

Shared writing: the opening as the crowd gathers. Setting the scene.

Guided writing: continue your description of the event.

The Entry of Christ into Prescot
(with apologies to Adrian Henri)

Bright Mersey morning, crisp packets fluttering
down Eccleston Street.
The smell of Sayers, Greggs, Waterfields,
pasties, sausage rolls, CAKES.
The sound of schoolkids
rattling on about The Simpsons, Stevie Gerrard,
Wayne Rooney,
goals.
Then,
up the hill from Huyton,
the sound of kazoos,
chanting,
swaying banners: Hail Jesus.
Now the procession,
beating drums,
helicopters chattering in an azure sky,
TV reporters, the *Liverpool Echo*
asking when Jesus is going to release
his latest CD.

They're selling tee-shirts,
chips soaked in salt and vinegar,
burgers.
The air reeks with tomato ketchup, fried onions
and faith.

The crowd sways, presses, surges,
swings on past the Fusilier pub
where strawberry-nosed men
cross themselves and cheer.

Down towards St Helens
and into St James Road
ending up outside Whiston Hospital
where the man in white
does his miracles.
Maisie Jones walks for the first time
in fifteen years
and the Royal Liverpool School for the Blind
is now the Royal Liverpool School
for Seeing like a Hawk.

Evening
falls like like a soggy pizza.
Weary parents drag grousing toddlers
home to toast, pyjamas and cuddles.
I make my way back
to an appointment
with *Newsnight* and the sofa.

Structure of the lesson

Paragraph 1 (opening)

Describe the scene as the crowds gather. Build a sense of anticipation. What kind of people gather at such events? What vendors are on hand? Use your senses (e.g. the tang of vinegar on the fish and chips, the odour of hotdog and onions). What do the salespeople shout to sell their wares? Think about the press, the police. Describe vividly (e.g. flashbulbs, the clatter of helicopter rotor blades).

Jesus comes to Prescot

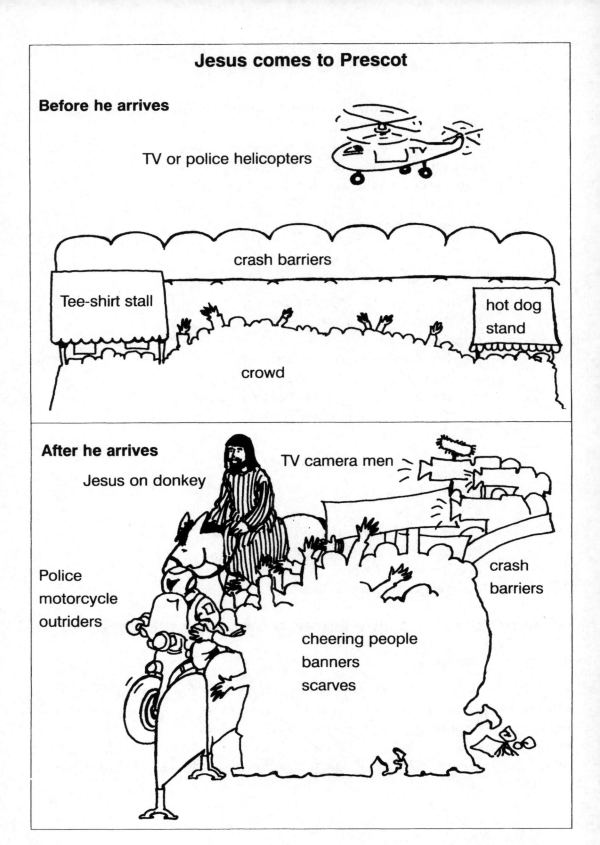

Before he arrives

TV or police helicopters

crash barriers

Tee-shirt stall

hot dog stand

crowd

After he arrives

Jesus on donkey

TV camera men

Police motorcycle outriders

crash barriers

cheering people
banners
scarves

Paragraph 2 (problem)

Jesus appears in the distance. What is he wearing? What effect does his approach have on the crowds (e.g. cheering, waving banners, holding up children)? Think who else will be present: police outriders, TV reporters, etc. Describe the press of the crowd. Think what people might be saying.

Paragraph 3 (action)

Describe Jesus performing miracles. Where does this take place (e.g. town hall steps, church)? Who comes to be healed? What is their reaction? How does the crowd respond?

Paragraph 4 (resolution)

Now describe the scene as night falls and the crowds wend their way home. Discuss the tone – elegiac (e.g. the glow of streetlamps, falling rain, chip wrappers bowling along the street. Think of a last line which draws it to a satisfying conclusion (e.g. *A small part of me would never be the same again*).

Examples of children's work

The entry of Jesus Christ in Prescot

By Hollie, Year 4

At two o'clock crowds started to form outside of the church. Forming a long row up towards Woolworths. People were wondering what was going on. People were pushing barriers. Next to me a woman was shouting, "Hail Jesus" and the little girl at the other side of me had a Jesus badge. Behind me there were two men pushing to buy a Jesus T-shirt. In front of me people were arguing about what he looks like. There was a smell of chip fat and vinegar. People were shouting, "Buy your holy crosses £2.99." "Buy a Jesus T-shirt, get one free." And people were giving out confetti.

Then around 3 o'clock there was an outburst of cheering, people throwing hats, confetti everywhere and police surrounding the people. There were police helicopters above, guards surrounding the barriers, some people getting arrested amd everybody shouting with joy. People shouting, "Hallelujah! He's here! He's here!"

Then miracles started to happen. The donkey rode down Prescot. People shouting, "sign my autograph, my autograph." There was a disabled lady passing by and Jesus made a click and she started to walk. Everybody's grey hair turned to its normal colour and I got the shoes I'd always wanted. A flush of joy burst out my body. This was the best day of my life ever.

Finally the procession was over, police clearing up. Confetti blowing round in circles and the school girls giggling.

Comments

Hollie creates a lively image of this event in the reader's mind.

Older children might explore the following:

- Could you use real-life TV presenters, celebrities, reporters? Could you quote their words? What food would be on sale? How did it smell? What did the helicopters sound like?
- Exactly how did the crowd react? Did they press forward? Was there jostling? Did arguments break out?
- Describe the scene at the Town Hall. Did Jesus go on to perform miracles? How was that reported in the press?
- Could you turn the final paragraph about the walk home into an elegy of the deserted city streets?

Again, there are obvious cross-curricular opportunities:

- Martin Luther King comes to London
- Julius Caesar marches in triumph through Crewe
- Superman visits Manchester
- England parade the Rugby World Cup

Lesson 12

A Christmas story

Working title: *The night Santa crash landed*

Lesson Plan

Objective:	to write the story of a fantasy event.
Stimulus:	Christmas cards.
Sentence level:	sentence structure.
Shared writing:	story openings. How the sleigh goes out of control.
Guided writing:	continue the story building on the opening.

Structure of the lesson

Paragraph 1 (opening)

Choose a good opening sentence to build tension. Show how Santa crash landed and ended up in a snow drift. What verbs will you use to describe the fall of the sleigh (e.g. *plummet, spin, spiral*)? How will you describe the sleigh plunging into the snow (e.g. *The sleigh came to rest in a cascade of pure white snow*)? Choose lots of detailed description to build a picture in the mind of the reader. Possibly end with humour, Santa's Wellington boots kicking in the snowdrift.

Paragraph 2 (problem)

How does Santa feel as the reindeer vanish into the distance? Does he cry? Paint a picture in the reader's mind of Santa's dejection. You could describe tears running down his ruddy cheeks or his shoulders hunched in disappointment. Make it visual. Show, don't tell.

Paragraph 3 (action)

Describe how Santa goes looking for ways to deliver the presents. Who might he meet on the road? Does he get his hopes up, then have them dashed? What disappointments does he go through?

Santa's Crash Landing

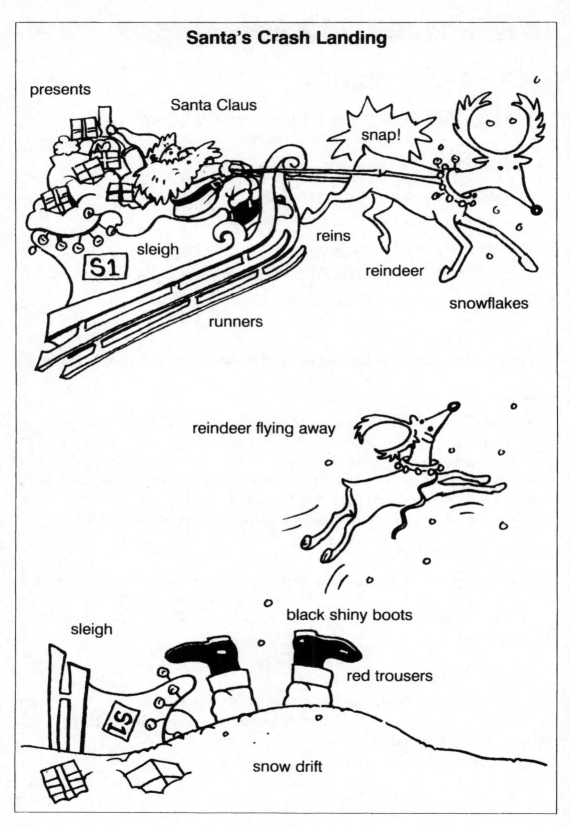

presents

Santa Claus

snap!

sleigh

S1

reins

reindeer

snowflakes

runners

reindeer flying away

sleigh

black shiny boots

S1

red trousers

snow drift

Can you think of a good ending? How does Santa finally solve his dilemma? How does he feel seeing the looks on children's faces? Make it visual (e.g. *He watched as Bobby's face was illuminated by the fairy lights*). How does his day end? Does Santa stand stroking his reindeer wondering where they've been all night? Does he book a holiday? (See Raymond Briggs' *Father Christmas*.)

Examples of children's work

The night Santa crash-landed

By Bethany Sharrock, Year 4

It was all going to plan when snap the reins broke out loose. Santa started to fall out. He shouted, "Come back, come back!" but the reindeers had already flown away into the distance. As Santa was falling the wind rushed past. He could hear leaves rustling. If he landed he would go head first. Then all of a sudden crash, bang, Santa fell down. He landed in a snow drift with his legs up in the air kicking up and down.

For several minutes tears ran down Santa's cheeks, until his cheeks were bright red, rosy. Santa was sitting down but then he stood up. He saw something in the distance. He thought he could see a sign saying helicopters to rent. So he ran, ran and ran for hours until … he came to the place. He said, "I know, I'll borrow one of them." He asked the man and the man said, "yes!" Santa hopped in, grabbed all his presents, pulled the lever and "Up, up and away," he said.

Finally Santa was delivering presents all over the world until, when he came to number 67, his big blooming bottom got stuck in the chimney.

Comments

Bethany's story is warm-hearted and funny. To extend this ask the children to consider the following:
- Can you make the most out of Santa himself? Did his usually cheery face drain of blood? Was his red suit damp and dirty?
- Could you describe his forlorn cries for the reindeer to come back?
- How did passers by react to a stranded Santa?
- Did he ever despair? Could you contrast the misery of Santa wondering how to deliver the presents with the joy of thinking up a solution?

Fiction is a series of *what ifs*. Pose the correct problems and the children's solutions will be effective and satisfying.

In the run-up to Christmas many children are offered a diet of word searches and colouring activities. Worthwhile English lessons are still possible, even when the hearty ring of Santa's laughter is in the air.

Other ideas in a similar vein might include:
- Where Santa goes on his holidays (see *Father Christmas Goes on Holiday* by Raymond Briggs)
- The true story of Rudolph the red-nosed reindeer
- How the Easter bunny discovered chocolate eggs
- The Snowman's story (once again see Raymond Briggs is the master. See *The Snowman*)
- Anancy the Spiderman and the Crocodile
- The story of Hanuman.

Lesson 13

A story based on experience

Working title: *The Den*

Lesson Plan

Objective: to write a narrative exploring a personal experience.

Stimulus: teacher's recollection of making dens as a child. Children's experiences.

Sentence level: sentence structure.

Shared writing: the opening. When did the writer first discover the place where they decided to build the den?

Guided writing: continue the story, describing building the den. Include a challenge (the den's destruction, the den being taken over by bullies). Conclude by considering how the child dealt with the challenge.

Structure of the lesson

Paragraph 1 (opening)

This kind of story does not rely on tension. Better to cut straight to the action. Where did you build your den? Was there an old hut already there or did you start from scratch?

Describe the surroundings. Was it deep in the woods? Was it in an old secret garden? Somewhere off the beaten track seems a good bet, away from the prying eyes of adults. It could be a tree house. It doesn't need to be direct personal experience. Most children would like a den even if they have never done more than hide under their bed!

Who were your companions?

Paragraph 2 (problem)

This paragraph concentrates on the exterior only.

What materials did you use to build your den? Where did you get them from? Describe the process of obtaining them. If it was hard work, say so.

The Den

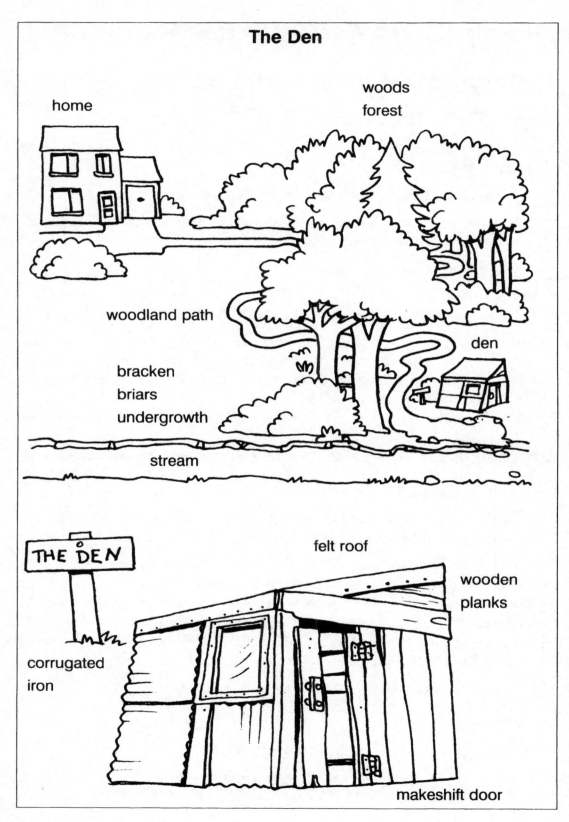

home

woods
forest

woodland path

den

bracken
briars
undergrowth

stream

THE DEN

felt roof

wooden
planks

corrugated
iron

makeshift door

How did you make the den waterproof? How did you secure the walls, the roof? Did you make an opening door?

How did your circle of friends behave? Did your little sister say she was bored? Did the dog run round barking?

Now go on to describe the interior (this could be an extra paragraph).

What did you put inside? Did you put up posters and pictures? Of whom? Did you get a piece of old carpet? Did you bring food in? What did you sit on? Did you have a torch?

Paragraph 3 (action/crisis)

One day something happens. It could be any of these:
• Bullies take it over.
• Builders put up a fence. They are going to build houses where the den is.
• Hooligans damage the den.

Describe the scene. Tell the reader how you felt.

Paragraph 4 (resolution)

How do you come to terms with what has happened? Do you rebuild the den or do you have to come to terms with the loss? Try to end the story with something positive:
• You get your den back.
• You learn to cope with things going wrong.

Think of a good, reflective last line.

Examples of children's work

The den

By Harry Tracey, Year 5

We built our den one summer's day. We found the best place deep in the woods. First we had to get some wood for the roof so we had to sneak into an abandoned warehouse and steal but nobody would care anyway. Next we had to make it waterproof so we went to a nearby tip and found some old waterproof coats. Finally we needed a few tools and nails. I took some from my Dad's tool box.

It took a long time to build but it was worth it. We had a few frights like spiders, owls and hitting each other on the thumbs with hammers and nails. Then we were finished.

The outside was great but the inside was special! It was a bit smelly but it would do. We built a lot of underground systems like toilets, circuits and special entrances to it. We got a T.V. (Sky), beds, couches, fridges, carpets and even trained a homing owl called Tom.

But to get all this came at a cost, exactly £30,000 but we never paid for it, just stole it. Later on we went home for a good night's sleep.

We came back to see a plague of butterflies invading the den – sitting on the couch, sleeping on the bed and eating all our food. We thought that was the end but it wasn't. I heard some sirens and lots of police came and arrested all of them. "You boys can have this, we found that they stole up to £30,000 in notes." So they drove off with the butterflies in the back and we got the den.

The den

By Hannah Perle, Year 5

On a bright summer's day, my friends Jack, Jessie, Shain, Danielle, Ricky, Rebecca and Joey all built a den. The den was made out of scaffolding and plastic covers, cement, old school chairs and plastic tubes. On top of the den was a huge hedge that had been cut down.

It was very strange. When I was younger it was decided that bungalows were to be built on the junk yard at the end of the road. We agreed when they brought huge buckets. We loaded the buckets with cement and took them to a secret garden that was full of ivy and it was hidden behind and underneath a huge field. We called it our own "SPBG". SPBG stood for SECRET PRIVATE BACKIES GARDEN. We got the scaffolding out of the huge junkyard where the builders had already dumped it. We worked as a team. We took turns on holding, fixing, glueing, placing, shouting, ordering and being in charge. The garden was underneath hundreds of layers of ivy. Nobody ever dared go into the SPBG without wearing trousers.

I haven't even started. We had tyre swings. We created our own theme park. Next door but one had lots of chunky thick rope. Our favourite ride was called the "Tyre top off". It was terrifying. It was the rope tied to each tree. You sat on a tyre and slid down the rope. It started off high and then went low. It was then caught on a branch. It spun you round until you were dizzy.

Danielle went sick, eww! All of our theme park was inside scaffolding cemented to the ground and huge plastic covers. Yes, there was a hole but within — miracles! — the inside was never wet. It was surrounded by Holly. It was also full of school chairs. Our SPBG has never been discovered.

Comments

The two pieces of work included here are distinctive and individual.

Harry's roars off into fantasy at times but is well told and engaging. Hannah's is full of the kind of detail ('the Backies') that tells you it was written in Kirkby, Merseyside.

In order to build on these first drafts the teacher could suggest:
• Could you make more of the musty smell of a den, the objects you would put inside it?
• Could you use lists to strengthen the descriptions?

Other ideas in the same vein might include:
• moving house
• a memorable holiday
• a sports event.

The important thing is that this is not autobiography. The children can draw on personal experience but they are fictionalising it.

Lesson 14

A time slip story

Working title: *Time slip*

Lesson Plan

Objective: to write a time slip narrative.

Stimulus: discussion of the idea of a time slip story. TV's *Dr Who*, *A Connecticut Yankee in King Arthur's Court* by Mark Twain, *Whose Side Are You On?* by Alan Gibbons, the Hollywood movies *Timeline* or *Back to the Future*.

Sentence level: using subordinate clauses; constructing complex sentences.

Shared writing: an opening designed to make the reader feel he/she is going back in time.

Guided writing: continue the story using the principle suspension of belief.

Structure of the lesson

Paragraph 1 (opening)

You need to get your reader's attention. Use the device of a digital wrist watch to show time going into reverse. What descriptive details can you employ (racing numerals, the watch throbbing on your wrist)? Next, show the room dissolving around you, or you fading from the room. Maybe you go through a time tunnel. What do you see (suns revolving across the sky; cities rising and falling)? What do you hear (roaring, screams)?

Paragraph 2 (problem)

Describe how you land (sprawling, crashing into a wall). Select a time to which you go back. In the case of the story shown below, it is ancient Egypt. First principle: don't give it away to the reader. Give them clues and make them guess where you are. Relate the clues to the time. Show your character slowly becoming aware that he has gone back to the past.

Paragraph 3 (action)

Now choose an exciting or humorous event. Your character is being walled up with other slaves to accompany the pharaoh into the afterlife. How do you feel? How do the other slaves react? Describe the scene in detail.

Paragraph 4 (resolution)

The children can choose their own ending, but this type of story suggests a cyclical ending returning to the first lines of the story. If you take this avenue the watch will begin to throb on your wrist, the numerals will race forward and you will fade from the burial chamber, reappearing in the present. How do you feel to be back?

Examples of children's work ∎∎∎∎∎∎∎∎∎∎∎∎∎∎

Timeslip

By Alex Mallon, Year 6

It all began with a digital watch. As I stared at the display the watch started to vibrate. The digits sprinted in reverse, slowly at first, then at breakneck pace. Out of the corner of my eye I glimpsed the world spinning me round. The walls began to fade. There, before my eyes, my skin became transparent then translucent. The world was crumbling before my eyes as buildings were built then dissolved. I stared with eager eyes.

Finally, the world came to a halt and I landed sprawling on the stony, sandy surface. For a moment I lay panting with desperate, anxious breaths.

I noticed my garments had turned into a light coloured tunic. The digital watch on my hand moments before had turned into an arm band and an amulet lay around my neck. I could feel something slithering around my foot as I saw a herd of scarabs. I plucked up the courage to discover hieroglyphs covering the bony corridors which lay in front of me.

I ventured a little further and to the horror of my ears I heard tramping feet. I realised, to my disbelief, I was to be one of those slaves. Tapestries hung before me as statues stole my fear away. A strange phenomenon stood in front of me dressed in a royal blue and rosy red gown. It seemed to me like a sarcophagus.

My attention was distracted by the bulging heavy slabs which were piling up behind me. I had a great deal of desperation to get out of here. I became reckless with misery as the stillness set. Suddenly I felt the familiar vibration coming back. As I stared down at my wrist a sense of relief ran through me as I noticed the time was racing forward.

The world blurred up again as I landed with a thump in the cold, wet, rainy night. At once I knew where I was – Britain, home sweet home.

Comments

Alex uses complex sentences and ambitious vocabulary, pacing the story well and guiding the reader towards the wholly satisfying ending. In one sentence the ambition doesn't quite come off. The teacher could demonstrate how a clause needs adding on line 4 to make the sentence work: 'There, before my eyes, as my skin became transparent then translucent, *I started to lose form, turn into a kind of human mist*.'

In this way, her ambition can be realised.

Throughout, teacher questioning can strengthen the effect:
• What did the vibration of the watch feel like?
• How did you react? Did you cry out when this strange event occurred?
• Could you describe the journey through time? Was there a vortex, a portal, a whirlpool of light? Did a thousand suns pass across the sky?
• When you arrive in ancient Egypt, imagine the sense of disbelief as you looked around. What objects did you say? Could you understand the other slaves in the burial chamber?
• Could you give more detail of the return home? This is an example of a cyclical rather than a linear narrative so the opening and ending of the story need to be in a very similar vein. Refer back to the opening directly in your resolution.

Other stories in this vein could be:
• going back to a Victorian schoolroom to be told off by a strict teacher
• becoming a Victorian chimney sweep engulfed in a fall of soot
• finding yourself in the Colosseum facing a gladiator or a wild tiger
• joining Boudicca to fight the Romans
• witnessing the sinking of the *Mary Rose* as a Tudor sailor
• fighting alongside Arthur against the Vikings

This kind of story can be written in a history lesson. It is a very useful vehicle for investigating history and for writing across the curriculum.

Lesson 15

A detective story

Working title: *Hostage*

Lesson Plan

Objective: to write a story in the detective fiction genre.

Stimulus: an excerpt from an old gangster movie or from an Anthony Horowitz story (for example, *The Falcon's Malteser*).

Sentence level: complex sentences.

Shared writing: a tension-building opening.

Guided writing: continue the story, taking your character through an old warehouse in search of a hostage.

Structure of the lesson

Paragraph 1 (opening)

Make the opening crackle with tension. You could see a dark figure, hear a muffled scream. What do you hear and see as you approach the warehouse (banging doors, the whistle of the wind, a guttering candle)?

How would your character react (shiver, check his gun)?

Paragraph 2 (problem)

Describe your character climbing the stairs. Again, what do you see and hear? Alert your reader to the possibility that the kidnapper is lurking in the warehouse. What clues can you drop (a cough, a shadow)?

Paragraph 3 (action)

Show your character entering the room. How do you turn the handle? Are you breathing heavily, sweating? Describe the hostage. How is he/she tied up? How do you know the kidnapper is in the room (the hostage's eyes widen? She struggles against her ropes)?

Describe the gunfight. Make it detailed. Not 'Bang, he's dead.' Show, don't tell.

Hostage

Exterior

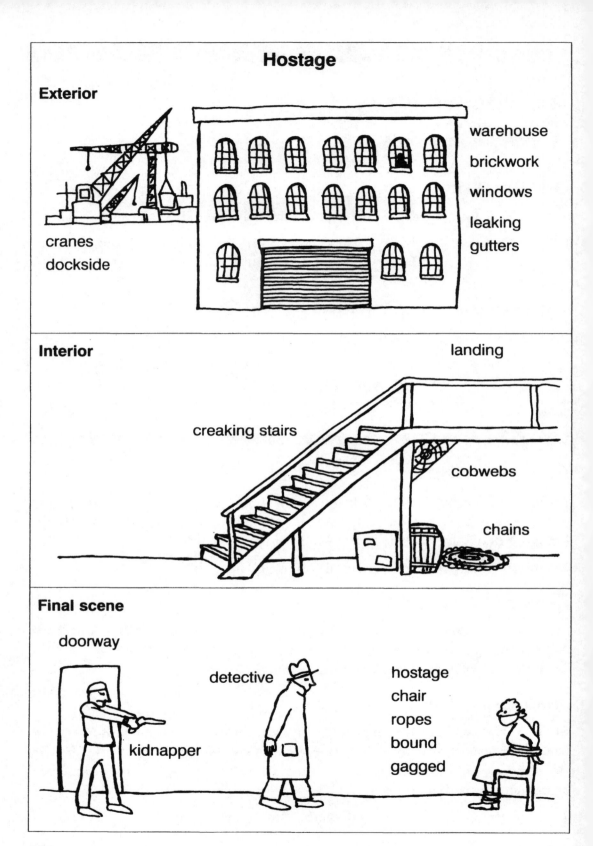

cranes
dockside

warehouse

brickwork

windows

leaking

gutters

Interior

landing

creaking stairs

cobwebs

chains

Final scene

doorway

detective

kidnapper

hostage
chair
ropes
bound
gagged

Paragraph 4 (resolution)

Try a twist in the tale. Is the gunman not dead? Does he rise again? Does he have an accomplice? How will you end the story to leave the reader feeling satisfied? Think about open and closed endings, reflections on what has happened.

Examples of children's work

The hostage

By Rachael O'Hare, Year 6

Somewhere in the building there was movement. Suddenly I heard a gust of wind rattling the shutters and rats scurrying along the floor. I heard muffled screams coming from inside the warehouse. I knew I had come to the right place. Uneasy and anxious, I stepped inside the old building. I felt cobwebs touch the side of my face. I reached for my gun. I opened the barrel to check how many bullets I had. Slowly I edged toward the stairs. I slowly slid up onto the first floor, then the second and finally the third. I very nervously crept toward the door.

I turned the handle and pushed the door forward wondering what lurked in the room ahead. Sweat ran down my face as I took my first step into the fatal room. I looked around carefully, expecting the kidnapper to be hiding somewhere, but no-one was there. No-one except the hostage, or so I thought. I took a few more steps into the room. Slowly I began to take the hostage's gag off. Suddenly the hostage began to nod her head as if to warn me of something. I turned around to see if anyone was there. There was. Quickly I ducked as the man behind me had a gun in his hand. I turned around and pretended to put my hands up. As I put my right hand slowly up I grabbed my gun. I shot one bullet at his arm then another at his chest. Slowly he fell to the ground dead.

I turned back around to release the hostage. As I finished taking her gag off I could tell she was relieved to be safe. I was proud of myself as I went home that night and was glad just to collapse on the bed.

Comments

Rachael writes confidently, building up an atmosphere with telling details (shutters, scurrying rats). She uses good sentence structures: 'Uneasy and anxious, I stepped inside the old building.'

Atmosphere is central to this kind of story. Everyone is familiar with the gumshoe in his mac and trilby hat. Using clips of Bogart films the teacher could suggest a dockland background. Figurative language helps: '*A foghorn brayed in the distance.*' The hero could show fright through telling details: '*I pulled up my coat collar.*'

The sentence at the end of Paragraph 1 doesn't work. Rachel could re-work it: '*Anxiety cascaded down my spine as I crept towards the door.*' Describe your hand on the door knob, the creak of the hinges. This all builds tension.

Finally, in the room, how does the detective know the kidnapper is behind him or her? Might they see him reflected in the eyes of the hostage? Could the hostage wriggle and writhe in her bonds? Might they make muffled sounds through the gag? Acting out a short piece of drama focuses the young writer on the process they are describing.

Internal monologue in the gumshoe style could also strengthen the story: '*This was the place all right. The tip-off was spot on.*'

Making the story work is all about building on the strengths in Rachel's story:
- description
- tension

A final element might be to look at the kind of aphorisms crime writers adopt. '*The kidnapper hit the floor like a sack of potatoes. The blood puddled round his head. I was safe, which was more than could be said of the sucker lying there on the deck.*'

Other ideas in this vein:
- cracking a safe
- tailing a suspect

Lesson 16

Mental mapping

Working title: *A mental map of Merseyside*

Lesson Plan

      Objective: to use mental mapping to write an account of place.

      Stimulus: a poster of features in the locality of the school; aerial photographs, etc.

Sentence level: connectives.

Shared writing: to open the piece of writing looking at items in the foreground.

Guided writing: to continue the story, looking at the middle ground and background.

Structure of the lesson

First, this is all about creating a sense of place, and second, it is about getting children to use the technique of addressing the reader directly. To make the stimulus of the lesson you could buy a souvenir tea towel of the locality, photocopy it and cut up the pictures. Paste them onto a poster sorting them into foreground, middle ground, background.

Draw attention to features which could be in each area:
- foreground – the district right in front of you or in the immediate vicinity of the school
- middle ground – the town beyond the immediate vicinity
- background – the surrounding countryside, hills, rivers

This will act as a visual stimulus for the pupil and also develop the structure within which to pace the writing.

Paragraph 1 (foreground)

Ask the children to examine the poster. What do they see in the foreground? Imagine the reader can't see these things. How can you describe them, creating a picture in the reader's mind? Use the phrase: *in the foreground* to get started. What do you hear, smell, see at each location? Use good adjectives and strong verbs to bring it to life.

103

Paragraph 2 (middle ground)

Use connectives to open Paragraph 2 (*now, next, after that*). Use phrases which involve the reader. Questions work well here (*Can you hear? Do you see?*) Then, once again, use good description to bring the place alive.

Paragraph 3 (in the background)

Discuss the connectives (*moving on, moving into the far distance, over on the far horizon*). Explore these features using the senses. Make it rich. Use proper nouns, places people will recognise. Not a bakery, but Gregg's, Sayers.

Paragraph 4 (resolution)

Use connectives (*finally, to conclude, last but not least*). Now ask the reader to colour in the picture in their mind. Use colours of association as well as at the literal level (the blue of Everton, the red of Anfield, the azure sky). Save the most evocative detail for the last line.

Examples of children's work

A mental map of Merseyside

By Mamie Dillon, Year 4

In the foreground I will paint the places I can see. In the Albert Dock I can see crowds of people exploding out of Anfield. In the mist I can see Birkenhead. The smell of drains. When I look up I see seagulls swooping down on the river.

Now let's close our eyes and listen. Do you hear the cry of seagulls? I can hear the sea rushing up against the boat. Can you hear the pouring water coming out of the drains?

Moving on, let's use our noses. Can you smell the sweet but bitter aroma of chocolate? Do you smell the chip fat and gravy coming from the chip shop down the road? I can smell hot doughnuts coming from Sayers.

Last but not least, let's colour it in. Look at the red of Anfield. Can you see the green seaweed of the sea? I can see the dark blue of the sky. The yellow submarine.

Comments

Mamie's writing immediately evokes Liverpool. It also uses complex sentences to effect: Can you smell the sweet but bitter aroma of chocolate?

The effect of the story relies upon two things:
* Vivid imagery. This Mamie provides in bucketloads.
* The linking sentences that provide a structure: *Moving on*, etc.

In order to develop this kind of writing the teacher could build up a series of 'toolboxes'. These are lists of useful connective sentences that draw the reader in and make them feel the narrator is addressing them directly.

For example:
* *Observe ...*
* *Picture ...*
* *Imagine ...*
* *Investigate ...*
* *Explore ...*
* *Let's examine ...*
* *Breathe in ...*
* *Enjoy the sights and sounds of ...*

This kind of phrase or sentence opening enables the young writer to lead their reader through the piece of writing.

This activity could be repeated with any place.

Cross curricular links with geography are obvious.

In history, you could use the idea of archaeology, dividing your poster into:
* Near the surface (recent times) you will find ...
* Below that (100 years ago) you will find ...
* Deeper still (hundreds of years ago) there is ...
* Finally, far, far below (before Mankind) explore ...

PART 3

A word on continuity and progression

Making progress

Sometimes, late in Key Stage 2 or early in Key Stage 3, you hear children complaining that they are repeating what they have already done. They can become bored and listless and feel that they don't seem to be learning anything new. Below I enclose a sample transition unit covering the last years of primary school and the early years of secondary school. This kind of planning does not need to be exhaustive or over-prescriptive. If teachers from the feeder schools met with their colleagues from the secondary schools once or twice they could draw up a simple transition unit for fiction, non-fiction and poetry. It would require a sample piece of work in each genre to be re-visited over a three-year cycle. This would give ample evidence of progression.

Sample transition lessons

Fiction

Year 6

Objective: to write a narrative, using techniques of tension and including metaphors and similes, personification.

Stimulus: discussion of ghost stories.

Sentence level: focus on units of meaning, indicating appropriate punctuation.

Guided writing: A ghost story

Structure of lesson
Paragraph 1 (opening/setting): the approach through the woods. Withold information to create tension.
Paragraph 2 (problem/complication): use personification to show the reader the house is haunted.
Paragraph 3 (action/crisis): entering the house. Reaching its evil heart. The house coming alive.
Paragraph 4 (ending/resolution): in the room with the evil creature at its hearts. Selecting an open or closed ending.

Year 7

Objective: to write a narrative, using techniques of tension and including metaphors and similies, personification. Also some dialogue

Stimulus: *Last train into Night* by Alan Gibbons.

Sentence level: focus on units of meaning, indicating appropriate punctuation.

Guided writing: A ghost story

Structure of lesson
Paragraph 1 (opening/setting): on the platform of a disused railway station. Withold information to create tension.
Paragraph 2 (problem/complication): the ghost train arrived. Imagery. Discovering it is haunted.
Paragraph 3 (action/crisis): a ride through the night. Discovering the secret of the haunting.
Paragraph 4 (ending/resolution): selecting an open or closed ending.

Year 8

Objective: to write a narrative, using techniques of tension and including metaphors and similies. Change of voice to second person.

Stimulus: *Walk with Me* by Alan Gibbons.

Sentence level: range of punctuation selected to address your audience directly.

Guided writing: A ghost story

Structure of lesson
Paragraph 1 (opening/setting): two characters, an evil narrator and an innocent reader he addresses. Building tension through hints.
Paragraph 2 (problem/complication): teasing the victim towards the house. Using personification to imply evil.
Paragraph 3 (action/crisis): trapped in the house. Building the tension.
Paragraph 4 (ending/resolution): determining a happy/unhappy ending. Is it open or closed?

A word on planning and assessment

The key question: who is planning for?

Teachers shouldn't plan because somebody tells them to. Blind acquiescence has never been the best foundation of pedagogy. They should do it in order to help the children they teach. They should do it in a way which is personal, idiosyncratic and purposeful to them. Ordinary teachers are all ordinary in the same way; good teachers are good in so many different ways. No doubt about it, over-prescriptive planning can actually distract from the process of teaching. Planning should be as simple and painless as it can possibly be, given the context in which teachers work. Teachers can be trapped in a vicious circle. They fill in endless planning sheets which they barely have time to consult. They mark the children's work and assess it. They start planning the next lesson, plucking the idea from a ring-bind folder. Finally they assess again. There can appear to be no rhyme or reason to this. It becomes an inchoate grind.

Instead of this vicious circle, one instantly recognisable to many teachers, I would suggest an alternative virtuous circle. You plan a sequence of lessons, all returning to the same central objective. This has the advantage of reinforcing the children's understanding by repeating the activity with a different stimulus. If every lesson is a one-off, if the curriculum is a scattershot system of plucking activities out of the air, or of extracting them from the curricular Bible of the day, children never get the chance to hone their skills. They flit from one activity to another without ever internalising the skills to which they are being introduced. I would suggest this model:

Lesson 1

Plan to write the first two paragraphs of a four-paragraph story. Visit the objective for the first time. Stress to the children that what is being prized is exploration, the development of new skills, quality not quantity. Mark and assess the activity, looking to highlight the next step for the child. Choose three pieces of work from children of different abilities. Decide what is the next step evidenced in each sample. Set differentiated objectives for the next lesson.

Lesson 2

Having used your assessment to inform your planning, put up each of the three pieces of work on the OHP. Give positive praise, indicating the strengths of each piece and using them to demonstrate good practice, then explain that if the writer tried this or that technique, he/she could make their work even better. Set each group an objective based on their own needs. The adults available to the teacher (TA, parent helper) should then rotate round the groups in the lesson cycle, directing their attention to each group in turn to ensure the children understand their own personal target and are addressing it.

Lesson 3

Return to the same genre. For example, if you have asked the children to write a ghost story in lessons one and two, try a werewolf story in lesson three. Some objectives may be the same, with the purpose of reinforcing what was learned. These could be:

- Show, don't tell
- The use of tension
- Figurative language
- Simile and metaphor

But don't stand still. Reinforce the children's knowledge but add one new element. Maybe you would like them to use subordinate clauses to make their sentences more resonant and memorable to the reader. This is grammar for meaning, grammar in context, and so much more satisfying than a decontextualised class exercise. Demonstrate what you mean.

Simple sentence: I crept forward through the darkness.
More complex sentence: Pulse throbbing, I crept forward through the darkness.

Simple sentence: In the garden I saw a figure.
More complex sentence: In the garden, strangely masked by the film of falling mist, I saw a figure.

Assess this new element. Once more, select a few pieces of children's work to illustrate success. Maybe show one which doesn't quite work and help the child get it right. Again you are using assessment to inform the planning of your next lesson.

Lesson 4

Use the OHP to look at the pieces of work. Use positive praise and demonstrate how to build on their success. Say things like: 'OK, Tony has done brilliantly here. There is one sentence where you've been very ambitious but I think you could tweak it to make it really work. Any suggestions?'

Make this element of the story from Lesson 3 the focus of your teaching in Lesson 4.

Look at the following two pieces of writing from Year 2 children. Both exhibit a good grasp of sentence structure and vocabulary. What targets could we set these children?

The Billy Goats Gruff

By Lauren Scott

On the bridge was a nasty troll. He had one googly red eye. He had bugs in his teeth. He had greasy hair. He had one ear like broccoli. His face was like an old granny's. He had skin like a stale apple. He climbed out and showed his sharp, greasy, green claws.

He shouted out, 'No one's allowed to cross my bridge.'

He says it every time when someone wants to get past.

The baby goat went onto the bridge.

'Please don't eat me. The next goat is bigger than me,' he said.

'OK then,' said the troll.

Then the next goat came onto the bridge.

'Please don't eat me. The next goat is bigger than me,' he said.

The next goat came.

'You can't eat me,' he said, and he kicked the troll in the air and he landed in Russia.

The goats munched the grass.

'Mmmm,' said all the goats.

The Billy Goats Gruff

By Ellie Reith

On the bridge was a troll. He had one red googly eye. He had red, greasy hair. He had one ear the size of a football. He had some bad, crooked teeth full of dead fleas. His mouth was as big as a fishing bucket. He climbed out and showed his big, slobbery, sharp claws. He jumped up and started to strike out with his claws and missed.

The little goat fled out of the way and he said, 'Please, please, don't hurt me. Let me cross the bridge and eat the sweet green grass. My big brother is coming. He is much bigger than me!'

So the little goat went across the bridge and gobbled the grass. It was better than awesome and the opposite of horrible. Meanwhile, at the bridge, the troll was waiting for the medium sized goat to go trip trap and he did and he had the same excuse as the little goat. Finally the big goat bucked up his horns into the troll and that was the last anyone had ever seen of him. For tea the goats had the best grass they had ever gobbled!

Lauren has no problem whatsoever with writing a coherent, correctly punctuated sentence. One thing you will notice in this excellent story is that she starts most sentences with the word 'He.' Fine, there's your objective next lesson. Demonstrate some alternative sentence starters:

- *With one googly red eye he watched the trolls.*
- *Snorting loudly, he climbed out and showed his sharp, greasy claws.*
- *What's more, he had skin like a stale apple.*

Lauren can then vary her sentence structures, giving texture and relief to her writing.

Ellie would similarly benefit from looking at sentence openings and connectives. There you go then, that's the objective sorted for this bright group in your next lesson. Get the teaching assistant to sit with them and ask them to use the odd sentence starter on their whiteboard to vary sentence structures. They can write them out and hold them up to be checked before transferring them to their books.

In this way, instead of hopping around, you are achieving a level of continuity and depth to your teaching. Each of the writing lessons that week builds on the previous lesson, steadily increasing your expectations of the children. Because the whole project is built on praise and demonstration, the children feel secure and able to take constructive criticism. What's more, planning and assessment are purposeful and ongoing, each informing the other.

By way of a conclusion

So that's my take on children writing fiction. The lesson plans aren't meant to be writing-by-numbers. They are one teacher's way of introducing youngsters to some structures, templates and triggers which help fiction to happen. They are designed to make young writers think about how a story works. But they are only one way of making a story work. There are many others. That is why you have to build choices, crossroads and pathways into your teaching, let the pupils go off in their own directions. And never stop searching for new stimuli, new ideas from the world of fiction to spark the young imaginations in your care.

In some ways being a teacher is a bit like being a parent. There is no easy way to let go. Send the kids off into the dark wood a day too early and they may end up in the belly of the Big Bad Wolf. Wait too long before you cut them loose and they are the wizened granny waiting for Red Riding Hood to call. That's right, you were so over-protective you forgot to teach them how to be an independent human being! It is all about professional judgement and that is a skill which is caught not taught. Just as you learn to write by writing, you learn to teach by teaching.

Every day I set off in search of my Holy Grail. I read books wherever I go. I even listen to audio books in the car. Let's face it, it's dead time if you don't do something with it. I immerse myself in good literature. More often than I care to admit I read a story and think: 'Why do I bother? I'll never write anything half as good!'

But, after a few hours of feeling sorry for myself, I'm back in the saddle. I don't plan my stories in great detail either. I consider myself a rock and roll writer. I get a hook-line, a riff, in the manner of Bruce Springsteen in 'Born to Run'. I see a few landmarks poking out of the mist. Then I let the story career down the hill like a boulder gathering snow on its way down the mountain. My only worry is that I might not catch it before it reaches the bottom.

Teachers shouldn't turn their lessons into straitjackets. Here are a few suggestions:
- Don't worry too much about handwriting, punctuation and spelling while the young writer is exploring language. At least, don't make it an obstacle to making things up. All that secretarial stuff is another department, a separate skill which needs addressing with rigour, but not always when you are writing the first draft of the story. Plus you can always use computers to tidy it up while the young writer watches.
- Don't rush the whole process. No real writer finishes a story in one session. They break off, think about it, even discuss it with another human being from time to time. Writers aren't *that* anti-social.

- Don't pretend there is a correct way to write a story. You can make up as many rules as you like. Some genius will always come along and break every single one.

All year round I watch serious, earnest youngsters riveted to the task of writing. I see the moral and spiritual growth that can come from story-telling. Then I get to wondering why it is an experience that passes so many young people by. The missing link, of course, is reading for pleasure. If there is one axiom I will have inscribed on my headstone, it is this:

'Read like a demon, write like a wild thing.'

Try my approach on your class. You have nothing to lose.

Bringing an author into school

Much of this book has been devoted to the notion of the teacher providing a model of the writing process, demonstrating to their students how to use language which is clear, expressive, imaginative, and even musical to communicate their ideas. There is, of course, another human resource which can be tapped and that is the writer.

Working with people who write for a living is a valuable experience. It demystifies writing and shows that it is something anyone can do. It demonstrates that expressing yourself through the medium of the written word can be both fun and emotionally rewarding. It helps introduce young people to the diversity and richness of contemporary British writing.

Writing Together is an initiative jointly organised by the Department for Education and Skills, QCA, Booktrust, Arts Council England and the Poetry Society. It is worth quoting at length from its publication *Bringing Writers into Schools*:

'Why a writer?

Inviting a writer into school:
- is inspiring and exciting for pupils and teachers
- encourages pupils to write and to see writing as worthwhile
- supports the teaching of both writing and reading
- pays dividends in pupils' development right across the curriculum, particularly in terms of planning, drafting and revising work
- encourages awareness of styles, imagery, structure and audience
- promotes the sharing of ideas and approaches
- helps young people to learn how inspiration is derived from a very wide range of sources
- provides a fresh awareness of the process and purpose of creative writing
- gives pupils the opportunity to think about how a book is created and where it all begins and ends
- promotes the idea of writing as a profession and writers as real people.'

Secretary of State for Education Charles Clarke says in the same booklet:
'Writing Together promotes creativity and raises standards because it brings together teachers, pupils and writers in a unique partnership. I am convinced of the value of writers in schools and look forward to these conferences developing effective approaches to writer visits and residencies so that they become a permanent part of the Key Stage 3 curriculum.'

For so many teachers who have often felt frustrated because of the pressures of a very prescriptive curriculum and testing regime, this can only come as a welcome statement. The only addendum I would make would be the Key Stage 1, 2 and 4 curriculums too.

Have clear objectives

It is important to have clear objectives. Do you want a long term or short term residence? What kind of writer do you want: a poet, a novelist, a non-fiction writer? With what age range will they be expected to work? Do you want them to give an author talk with questions and answers or would you like somebody who can lead writing workshops? Would the children benefit most from a mixture of the two? Will you incorporate sales of the author's books into the day? It should be self-evident that book ownership plays an extremely important part in encouraging young readers.

There are other considerations. What will be the outcome of the residence or visit? Will work be displayed around the school? Will it be published in an anthology or on the Internet? What follow-up will there be? Are parents or members of the local community going to be involved? Could you organise a celebration of achievement?

Find a suitable writer

Expect to pay a minimum fee of £250 a day, plus travel expenses and accommodation if required. Remember that writers have to earn a living too. For every J K Rowling, Jacqueline Wilson or Terry Pratchett there are hundreds of struggling writers. The Society of Authors estimates that 75% of authors receive an income comparable to a cleaner! This is a modest investment. Many schools invite several writers a year and their students gain a great deal from the experience. Information on funding can be found on the website of the National Literacy Trust: www.literacytrust.org.uk

Many authors have their own websites and you will be able to find out if they do school visits. You can also find writers who have experience of working in schools by contacting Booktrust, the Poetry Society, the National Association of Writers in Education or the various regional databases (information below). Your local library may also arrange visits by authors. Building a relationship with the library should be central to the ethos of the school anyway. The Artscape directory ensures that all individuals listed have enhanced disclosure checks from the Criminal Records Bureau and appropriate insurance.

Allow plenty of time between the initial contact and the visit. Many writers, especially those who have appeared on the shortlists of the many book awards, tend to be booked six to eight months ahead. I have lost count of the number of schools who have called me in February to ask if I can come on World Book Day in March. I usually answer: 'Which March?'

Practical advice

Agree the total cost, including travel and accommodation, well in advance. Check whether the author is VAT registered. If possible, arrange for the cheque to be ready on the day. If this is impractical, give the writer a rough idea when they can expect payment. The penniless writer waiting for a cheque to come in the post isn't completely fiction.

Have a clear line of communication: a phone number or email address. Arrange for the author to be picked up if they are coming by public transport. If they are driving, make sure they have a map and clear directions well in advance.

Negotiate the timetable of events with the writer. Don't spring a list of demands on them on arrival. This will only cause tension. Discuss the room in which they will work and check what equipment they will need. Do your best to avoid interruptions. Dragging children out of an engrossing session to see the dentist or attend an assembly is hugely frustrating and counter-productive.

Make arrangements for breaks and for lunch. The author should be provided with a bottle of spring water during sessions. Coffee and biscuits during breaks always go down well. Lunch should be provided. Check dietary requirements in advance. Don't expect the writer to fend for him or herself. Remember, they are in unfamiliar surroundings. We all need a little TLC. I heard of one famous poet who asked for a school lunch. He was told no and had to eat fish and chips on the sea front!

Prepare the children in advance. They should be familiar with at least one of the writer's titles. It helps to have looked up the author's website. Do your homework. I was once introduced to 200 Year 8s as follows:

'This is...what was your name again? ... Right, this is Mr Gibson ... What ... Oh, Gibbons! I'm afraid I haven't read any of your books, but teachers are busy people. Well, this is Year 8. Off you go.'

Make sure the writer is supported at all times. Don't leave them alone with 32 children. Don't do your marking at the back. Get involved. Working with a writer acts as INSET. What's more, it is enjoyable and enriching.

Contact the local media to publicise the visit. It is good for the school, good for the writer and good for the pupils.

Useful contacts

Arts Council England
14 Great Peter Street,
London,
SW1P 3NQ

Tel: 0845 300 6200.

Arts Council England is the national development agency for the arts in England. It distributes public money from Government and the National Lottery.

Scottish Arts Council
12 Manor Place,
Edinburgh,
EH3 7DD .

Tel: 0131 226 6051.

Website: www.scottisharts.org.uk

Arts Council of Wales
9 Museum Place,
Cardiff,
CF10 3NX

Tel: 02920 376500.

Website: www.artswales.org

Arts Council of Northern Ireland
MacNeice House,
77 Malone Road,
Belfast,
Northern Ireland.
BT9 6AQ

Tel: 028 9038 5200.

Website: www.artscouncil-ni.org

Academi
3rd Floor,
Mount Stuart House,
Mount Stuart Square,
Cardiff,
CF10 5FQ

Website: www.academi.org

Academi promotes literature in Wales. It runs a literary award, has a directory of writers and funds author visits.

Booktrust
45 East Hill,
London
SW18 2QZ

Tel: 020 8516 2977

Email: info@booktrust.org.uk

Website: www.booktrust.org.uk
             www.booktrusted.com

Booktrust is an independent educational agency. Among other initiatives it coordinates National Children's Book Week, publishes the magazine Booktrusted News for teachers and organises the Booktrust Teenage Prize.

The National Association of Writers in Education (NAWE)
PO Box 1,
Sheriff Hutton,
York,
YO60 7YU

Tel: 01653 618429

Email: info@nawe.co.uk

NAWE is a membership organisation which supports teachers and writers interested in creative writing in educational settings. It organises conferences, a magazine *Writing in Education* and an Internet directory of writers and artists who work in schools.

NAWE membership is £20 per annum.

The Poetry Society
22 Betterton Street,
London,
WC2H 9BX

Tel: 020 7420 9894.

Website: www.poetrysociety.org.uk

Email:
education@poetrysociety.org.uk

The Poetry Society has a lot of valuable experience of organising visits and residencies and offers a consultancy service.

Apples and Snakes
Tel: 020 7738 0941

Email: jasper@applesandsnakes.org

Website: www.applesandsnakes.org

Apples and Snakes promotes performance poetry and can arrange workshops and performances.

The Arvon Foundation
Tel: 020 7931 7611

Email: b.lyon@arvonfoundation.org

Website: www.arvonfoundation.org

The Arvon Foundation runs residential writing courses at its centres.

Book Communications
116 The Custard Factory
Gibb Street,
Birmingham,
B9 4AA

Tel: 0121 246 2777, 0121 246 2770.

Email:
jonathan@bookcommunications.co.uk

Book Communications runs a major writers-in-schools programme, 'Write On', working with seventy schools a year in the West Midlands.

PEN – Readers and Writers
Website:
www.englishpen.org/readersandwriters

Tel: 020 7713 0023

Readers and Writers brings writers in direct contact with readers of all ages and backgrounds.

Royal Festival Hall Literature Education
Tel: 020 7921 0867

Email: sasha@rfh.org.uk

Royal Festival Hall Literature
Education organises a range of
projects to promote contact with
writers and artists.

The Windows Project
Liver House,
96, Bold Street,
Liverpool
L1 4HY

Tel: 0151 709 3688.

Email:
windows@windowsproject.demon.
co.uk

Website:
www.windowsproject.demon.co.uk

Since 1976 Windows has worked with
schools and school groups in libraries
bringing libraries and school students
together.

New Writing North
7-8 Trinity Chare,
Quayside,
Newcastle upon Tyne,
NE1 3DF

Tel: 0191 232 9991

Email: mail@newwritingnorth.com

Website: www.newwritingnorth.com

This writing agency organises long
term residencies by poets; creative
writing summer schools; writing
courses for teachers and governors;
writers' roadshows into schools; work
with Education Action Zones.

Poetry Can
Unit 11, Kuumba Project,
Hepburn Road,
Bristol
BS2 8UD

Tel: 0117 942 6976.

Email: info@poetrycan.demon.co.uk

Poetry Can helps involve people in
poetry activities in the Bristol area.

Bibliography

Books by Alan Gibbons

Upper KS2 and KS3

THE LEGENDEER TRILOGY *(all published by Orion)*
Shadow of the Minotaur
Vampyr Legion
Warriors of the Raven

THE JULIE AND ME BOOKS *(all published by Orion)*
Julie and Me and Michael Owen Makes Three
Julie and Me: Treble Trouble

RECENT NOVELS *(all published by Orion)*
The Dark Beneath
Caught in The Crossfire
The Edge
The Lost Boys' Appreciation Society
The Defender

THE TOTAL FOOTBALL SERIES *(all published by Orion)*
Some You Win
Under Pressure
Divided We Fall
Injury Time
Power Play
Last Man Standing
Twin Strikers
Final Countdown

YOUNGER NOVELS *(all published by Orion)*
Chicken
Ganging Up
Playing With Fire
Whose Side Are You On?
Dagger in the Sky
Not Yeti

Books for younger readers (KS1, early KS2) *(All published by Collins Pathways)*

When My Ship Came In
Grandad's Ears
Hattie Hates Hats
Climbing Boys
City of Fire

Books for reluctant readers (KS1, early KS2) *(All published by Barrington Stoke)*

The Cold Heart of Summer
The Night Hunger

Books and magazines about writing and children's books

On Writing by Stephen King (Hodder and Stoughton)

Did I Hear You Write? By Michael Rosen (Andre Deutsch)

My Grandmother's Motorbike by Pie Corbett and Brian Moses (OUP)

The Trouble with Boys by Angela Phillips (Harper Collins)

Books for Keeps magazine (6, Brightfield Road, Lee, London SE12 8QF)

Carousel magazine (Saturn Centre, 54-76 Bissell Street, Birmingham B5 7HX

ACHUKA Internet site: www.achuka.co.uk

Young Writer magazine (Glebe House, Church Road, Weobley, Hereford, HR4 8SD)

Meetings with the Minister, essays by Bernard Ashley, Chris Powling, Jamila Gavin, Philip Pullman and Anne Fine (National Centre for Language and Literacy, www.ncll.org.uk)

Finally you can contact Alan Gibbons through his website www.alangibbons.com